SPRINGING
THE TIME TRAP

Other Books by Deniece Schofield

Confessions of an Organized Homemaker
Confessions of a Happily Organized Family
Kitchen Organization Tips and Secrets

SPRINGING THE TIME TRAP

Time Management for Today's Busy Homemaker

DENIECE SCHOFIELD

*This book is dedicated to McDonalds and
to my marriage. To McDonalds in loving
appreciation for feeding my family every
Tuesday night with their two-for-one
specials. And to my marriage, which has
somehow survived despite the fact that I've
written four books.*

©1987 Deniece Schofield
Printed in the United States of America

First printing August 1987
Second printing February 1989
Third printing September 1993
Fourth printing January 1997
Library of Congress Cataloging-in-Publication Data

Schofield, Deniece, 1947–
    Springing the time trap.

    Includes index.
    1. Home economics.   2. Women—Time management.
I. Title.
TX147.S37   1987   640'.43   87-16278
ISBN 0-87579-100-X (pbk.)

Contents

v

Introduction

Have you ever heard anyone say, "I wish I had spent more time on my business?" Neither have I. Curious then, isn't it, that so many books have been written about success, winning, and time management in business. After all, who needs the most help—a businessman who receives his mail in priority order from a swarm of skilled secretaries or a busy mother who doesn't even think about her mail until two hours before bedtime?

I have a hard time feeling sorry for the poor business manager who dines on a power lunch of sushi and sparkling Perrier water. Oh sure, I can have a power lunch, but chances are I'll have to clean up after it, too. More than likely my power lunch consists of a peanut butter and jelly sandwich and a handful of corn chips. The power part comes in when I discover how many errands I can run while I'm eating.

Like it or not, homemakers are now the ones who need help with time management. If we work outside our homes, we have *two* full-time jobs, and if we're full-time homemakers, no one has to tell us that we have all the work we can handle. So where do we turn for help?

Time-management experts haven't totally forgotten us. They're always kind enough to offer a few paragraphs of advice that, boiled down, consist of the following: "These same principles can also be translated into use at home." Thanks a lot!

When a businessman needs help, he goes to a morale-building pep rally, a convention, or a seminar. And after a hectic day at the office, he returns home to recline in an easy chair and prop up his feet while he unwinds.

Homemakers are the ones who, without the aid of computers, a pool of secretaries, or business consultants, have to sort through the socks, pancakes, and paychecks; the dust, the dishes, and the term-paper deadlines. Yes, we're the ones who need the help, the hints, and the motivation. That's why I have written this book. It is for kindred spirits who, like me, have hit bottom. If your experience is similar to mine, your kindling is a little damp. Here's what I mean. Check the following list and see if any of these time-management problems sound all too familiar:

1. Your driveway is a veritable minefield of kiddie toys: Big Wheels, psychedelic-colored skateboards, basketballs, Happy Meal sandpails, and all the trappings for Ken and Barbie's next date.

2. Your house looks as if Rambo is doing the housework.

3. Your laundry schedule is similar to this: Do all the washing on Monday. Pile clean laundry in a corner until Saturday, then fold it and put it away.

4. Your days are a continual round of, "Hey you!" "I need!" "I want!"

5. Your civic involvement amounts to voting in most of the presidential elections.

6. Procrastination has been the mother of invention on more than one occasion. For example, on Halloween you pass out the candy your kids have collected. Ten minutes before dinner, you survey the pantry and wonder if you can whip up something wonderful out of cream of asparagus soup, overripe bananas, and Paul Newman popcorn. And when your kids are invited to a birthday party, instead of remembering to pick up a gift you send three dollars in a plain white envelope.

7. You are considering renting a U-Haul storage shed to hold your unfinished projects.

8. You wonder if the kitchen counter is the devil's answer to flypaper.

9. Your exercise program consists of watching Jane Fonda's Workout videotape while you eat breakfast.

10. You handle floating scraps of paper in one of three ways: your left hip pocket functions as your "in" basket and your right hip pocket as your "out" basket; your refrigerator is a collage of magnetized memoranda; or your bulletin board is awash with layers of vital, although outdated and ready-to-be interred, information.

Thirteen years ago, discouraged, overwhelmed, and about nine miles east of hopeless, I hit bottom. I answered "Yep, that's me" to *all* of the above. Had I known the warning signals of "malignant management"—fatigue, stress, frustration, constant interruptions, guilt, feelings of inferiority, depression, lack of time, feelings of being overwhelmed, and discouragement—perhaps I could have arrested the disease in its early stages.

Luckily, I won the fight against my malignancy. But the road to recovery wasn't easy. I read book after book about time management; I attended time-management seminars and listened to stacks of tapes on the subject. I spent a fortune on calendars, each one promising to be the elusive cure. I observed good managers and asked a lot of questions. Generally, I discovered that the world's approach to time management is backwards. Yes, books are written and seminars orated to promote successful management and productivity on the job. So what's wrong with that? I'll tell you what's wrong.

I truly believe, with Samuel Johnson, that "to be happy at home is the ultimate aim of all ambition." Think about that for a minute. Why do people slave away at their chosen professions day after day, week after week, decade after decade? Isn't the real reason so they can have comfortable, contented homes? That's certainly why *I* am a member of the chain gang. So here is where the backwards approach comes in. Though corporations spend millions to teach their employees how to become productive, ultimately we're all working to be happy at home. Right? Then why not teach people how to do just that. Let's learn how to manage well and become productive at home first. Then when we hit the workplace, the corporations will automatically become better managed and more productive.

Case in point: When we leave home in the morning knowing the house is straightened, the laundry is folded and put away, and dinner is ready to pop in the oven, we can literally fly through the rest of the day. We're more pleasant on the phone, we handle stressful interruptions better, we think faster, and, in short, we turn out high-quality work. Contrast that with the days we stumble out of bed, bark out orders to the family, search for shoes, tape together ripped-up homework, and leave the cereal dishes to petrify on the kitchen table. During that day we accomplish maybe half of our potential.

Now, don't expect to see me on talk shows espousing this theory. Corporations will never buy it. Why? There's no money in it. Most time-management seminars, cassette tapes and courses are priced for the elite few. Most of us can't afford the high price of this education without corporate money to foot the bill.

So, off my soapbox. My mission in writing this book is to show you how to get things done at home—how to manage your home, nurture your family, and still have time and energy left for personal development. In other words, time for you.

Sound too good to be true? Mission impossible? No! This is a Charles Atlas course for the timid time manager, the one who's been bullied, knocked down, and dragged out by old Father Time.

During my desperate days I was the perpetual victim. With three boys under four, a puppy named Schoey Ralph (who had a penchant for chasing motorcycles), and a washing machine that headed south whenever it was running, I was always at the mercy of my environment. At this point in my life I was following an innovative method for managing my time. Actually it was a two-pronged approach: badgering and complaining.

One day, having reached the "enough already" point, my husband, Jim, sat me down and said, "Deniece, there are millions of other people out there who have more children than you have, more animals, and no washing machines. Some of them have physical impairments; some work outside their homes and are away ten hours a day; and many are doing all this without a spouse or a network of friends and relatives. And yet, in spite of the odds, they somehow manage their time and their surroundings very well and accomplish more in one day than many disorganized folks accomplish in ten years. Now, with all your capabilities and all the resources you have at your fingertips, I KNOW YOU CAN DO IT TOO."

That scene was not, as you may have guessed, the turning point in my life. I didn't reach that point until two weeks later. You see, it was then that I stopped reacting (with hate, defiance, hurt, and anger) and started thinking about what he had said. My own pride was choking me, and I knew in my heart that he was right. So, do as I did: stop stewing and start doing. *You* can do it too. How can I be so sure? The fact that you're holding a book in your hands that was written by *me* is proof enough. Here's the story.

When I hit the nadir of my career as a housewife and decided to shovel my way out of the mess, I kept at it. Sometimes I felt as if I were bailing water with a thimble, but nevertheless, I kept bailing. After weeks of hard work and diligent effort (not to mention four trips to the dump, eight donation drops to the Salvation Army, and two letters from same stating, "We're needy, not desperate"), I was ready to let family and friends see the new me and the blissful state of our organized existence.

We took the "House Out of Order" sign off the front door and started inviting people over to visit. Without fail, just as our unsuspecting guests prepared to leave, Jim would jump up and say, "Wait! Come in here and see how Deniece has organized our games. Isn't this a great idea?" Well, our visitors were always very kind and said (with raised eyebrows and winks to each other), "Oh, yes, Jim—great ideas." With such encouragement, before long he would have every closet, cupboard, drawer, cedar chest, and storage box in the house opened for full view and inspection.

Well, it only took a few polite guests to convince Jim that we were onto something. "Deniece," he said one day, "you should write a book. Put all these ideas down on paper."

This plan was so utterly preposterous I wouldn't even justify his remarks with a reply. But as the months went on and the nagging intensified, I began planning my counterattack. I knew I couldn't write a book, and somehow I had to convince Jim. Finally, after yet another "write a book" prodding, I said, "Jim, I cannot write a book. Here is the conclusive evidence I have collected that will prove once and for all that I am incapable of authorship:

"1. I have no credibility. After all, what right do *I* have to teach anyone else how to organize and manage their homes?

"2. Everyone else already does all the things I'm doing. For the past few years, I've been catching up with the rest of the world. (P.S. I honestly believed this!)

"3. I have never taken a writing course in my life. I don't know how to write a story, let alone a book.

"4. It is impossible to find a publisher. There are millions of authors out there—real writers—who know how to write and have something important to say. Many of them can't get a publisher to buy their books. Now, how do you suppose I—with no experience, know-how, or relative in the business—can ever be published? This whole idea is incredible.

"5. I have four kids and another one on the way. I don't have time to write a book."

Now I ask you, Aren't those wonderfully valid reasons for not writing a book? I think my argument was very convincing, logical, and, above all, accurate. But as if I had said absolutely nothing, Jim continued with his haranguing telling me, "You can do it. I know you can."

Enter plan B. The only way to convince this man, I thought, is to write a manuscript, give it to him, and let him fall flat on his face. Tough love, I think they call it. So that's exactly what I did. I wrote a manuscript, handed it to Jim, and said, "Here. Now leave me alone. This will prove I cannot write a book." He said, "Thank you very much," and here I am with book number four.

If I could learn how to manage my home, nurture my family, and still have time for me (let alone write a book about it), so can you. Yes you can, if—and here's the kicker—*if* you have the desire. Wasn't it desire that took a klutz like me and formed me into a manager? Yes, it takes desire. Without desire, you'll never pay the price for your dreams.

Stop the rushing, the disorganization, and the chaos. Begin to enjoy an easy, ongoing program to help you achieve the quality of time you want in your life. You can do it. You have the desire, or you wouldn't be reading this book. I know, you don't have time to read. But won't you pay the price?

1

The Hurried-er I Go

Take Time to Plan

I can pick them out in a crowd every time. Yes, world-class time managers are easy to spot just by looking through their handbags. For the most part their bags are usually on the small side and contain only the bare essentials. Their checkbooks are balanced and do not have fat rubberbands wrapped around them to keep junk from falling out. There's no sign of grocery ads, earrings, ticket stubs, empty Binaca atomizers, Slurpee straws, or shopping lists. (And yes, all rubber noses, green make-up base, and plastic spider rings are removed within three days after Halloween.)

Whenever I give a workshop, I do a lot of surreptitious handbag sleuthing. As the unsuspecting participants arrive, I glance at their handbags. And what handbags they are! Tote bags, satchels, miniature golf bags, bags the size of Hoover attachments, shoulder bags so heavy they could throw your hips out.

And what do people put inside these prodigious carry-alls? In order to unravel the mystery, I offer a prize to the woman who can remove the most disgusting piece of garbage from her bag. Frankly, I've seen everything. *National Geographic* wrapper, baby bootees, chewed gum, an empty tube of ointment, an expired library card, hair curlers, rocks, school papers, brown paper sacks, and a grocery list. A grocery list? Big deal, you say? Ah, but this particular one had been used in desperation to wipe a runny nose! Not to be upstaged, one woman had part of her single sock collection. There's a logical explanation, however. She was making a quilt out of the socks and needed to pick up some matching thread.

Trust me. Incredible though it seems, you *can* spot experienced time managers by looking through their handbags. Just for fun, grab your own bag, dump the contents on the kitchen table, and have a look. Before you start sifting through and analyzing the medley, though, take a minute and throw out all the soiled Kleenex tissues, candy bar and gum wrappers, cash register receipts, and the Cheerios you took to church to keep the kids quiet. We want to get right to the nitty gritty.

Now, if time management is a problem for you, you're likely to find some interesting (and very revealing) stuff in your handbag. If you dig up such things as the buttons for your daughter's Easter dress (don't fret—maybe your younger daughter can wear it if you finish it by next Easter), the envelope with Aunt Betty's new address on it, the recipes you got at last month's Tupperware party, and a receipt from the dry cleaners for the tie that's been missing nigh unto seven months, your days don't exactly begin with a flourish and a pat on the back, do they.

Yes, from the contents of your handbag you can tell to some degree whether you're a finisher or a dreamer; a manager or a firefighter; a doer or a forgetter. Please don't assume that I'm pointing an accusing finger. I've had one of those handbags too, but I've discovered what it takes to be a time-management winner, and I want to share that discovery with you.

Before I understood the importance of governing my time, there were many days when my home was well managed; there were days when my family was nurtured; there were even a few days when I enjoyed some personal development. But as I tried to juggle the three, I could never keep all the balls in the air at the same time. One or two were always lying at my feet. It was like trying to have ten great-looking fingernails at the same time. On the days I enjoyed personal development, the house looked like a nuclear test site. Ditto on the days I spent nurturing my family. I desperately wanted to manage, nurture, and develop simultaneously every single day.

Though my intentions were noble, instead of taking command at the driver's seat, I was under the rear wheels. It wasn't until I did some introspective soul searching that I discovered the source of my dilemma. Often the first step toward a cure is accepting that a problem exists. Actually, I discovered that several problems existed. I had been virtually powerless to change my behavior because I was relying on many inaccurate assumptions that I regarded as facts. Here are the five reasons why I was not managing my time. See if any of these same reasons apply to you.

Reason Number One: I do not want to become a clock-watching robot.

Some people assume that if they are managing their time well, they automatically qualify as type A personalities: aggressive, self-centered, rigid, impatient, hypertense, aloof, and premeditated. Admittedly they get a lot done, but the body count is long and grisly. So, for fear of bringing on a rise in blood pressure and a drop in popularity, such people continue their old habits of plodding along through life, letting each day unfold as it goes along.

For years I subscribed to this theory, refusing to be as rude and impertinent as I suspected all time managers really were. That was, however, until I met Charles R. Hobbs, world-renowned time-management expert and author. I remember vividly my first meeting with Charles. As the hour of my appointment drew near, the rate of my pulse increased. You see, anyone with letters after his name (his are Ph.D.) is immediately intimidating to me. Compounding my fears was the fact that this lettered man was a time-management expert. I left for my appointment several minutes early, knowing that being late would be the kiss of death. Gripping the steering wheel with white knuckles, I prepared myself mentally for our meeting. I imagined a very cold reception by an extremely efficient secretary who would tersely announce my arrival. At the exact appointed hour I would be ushered into Dr. Hobbs's office, where he would be waiting to dispense with me so as to score another check mark on his long to-do list.

By the time I was on my mettle, ready to face the "Grim Reaper," I had pulled up in front of Dr. Hobbs's office building. I took ten deep breaths, swallowed hard a few times, and walked up to the front door.

Imagine my surprise when Dr. Hobbs himself greeted me with one of the warmest and most sincere welcomes I have ever received. I was not, as I had fantasized, rushed briskly into his private office; rather I was introduced to his entire staff, who in turn acted as if this introduction was the highlight of their day. *Can these people really be time managers?* I mused.

Dr. Hobbs's office was also a surprise—comfortable and inviting, with not a clock to be found. His desk was absolutely bare except for his planning notebook. This man was, I discovered, the epitome of what a time manager should be.

I had many items to cover on my agenda, and Dr. Hobbs gave me all the time I needed. By the time I left, I felt that all my questions had been answered, all my needs met. For over an hour I had had Dr. Hobbs's undivided attention. His secretary didn't stick her head in the door to remind him of a more important meeting; his phone was silent; he was not the least bit condescending; and, incredibly, he never looked at his watch. Imagine, a time-management expert who didn't even look at his watch!

Reason Number Two: Planning wastes time.

"My time is so limited, a ten-minute planning session would just put me ten minutes behind. I'd rather just get started now." This sounds logical enough, but I've had enough holes poked in my umbrella to teach me otherwise.

Years ago I was asked to teach a Sunday School class of five-year-olds. Feeling fairly competent with the subject matter, I waited until late Saturday evening to look over the lesson plan. Then, as I glanced through the list of materials required, I discovered I needed a picture of Jesus feeding the 5,000, with a copy for each child to color. By that time all the photocopy offices in our town were closed, and my only recourse was to travel twenty minutes to find a photocopier. I spent the better part of an hour accomplishing something that would have taken less than five minutes had I done it during the course of a normal work week. But I didn't have time to plan.

Late one afternoon, with the dinner hour fast approaching, as usual I had no idea what I was going to fix. After a spot check of cupboard shelves, I decided I could prepare enchiladas. Bustling with activity, I soon had the meat and beans browned and simmering in the frying pan, with the sauce bubbling and thickening in a saucepan. I felt somewhat smug that I had pulled this entire meal off without even so much as a forethought, as I assembled the casserole and put it into the oven. All I had left to do was to grate the cheese and put some sour cream into a serving dish.

If you're one step ahead of me, you already know that we didn't have any cheese or sour cream, and to eat enchiladas without either one or the other would be unthinkable. With only a few minutes to spare, I checked with my neighbors, who either weren't home or were not any better stocked than I. My only recourse was to make a quick dash to the grocery store.

I turned off the oven, grabbed the kids, hustled down the road to the closest market, parked the car, bulldozed the children into the store, and picked up the cheese and sour cream. On the way to the check-out counter I ran into a friend whose child was a "co-partner in crime" with my rambunctious third grader. After ten minutes or so of commiserating, we said our good-byes and I made my way to the end of a very long line of anxious shoppers. By the time I reached home, forty-five minutes and my good nature had expired. This whole scene could have been avoided had I spent ten minutes planning menus before I did my weekly shopping. But, alas, I didn't have time to plan menus.

On another occasion, one of my children rushed into the house after school, calling, "Hey, Mom! Can you drive me to the library tonight? I have to do a report about Ernest Hemingway and it's due tomorrow." Reluctantly I agreed to this request, wishing that one day this child would quit procrastinating. (I assumed he must have picked up this bad trait from his father.) "You've just got to learn to plan ahead," I declared.

We drove to the library and fortunately found three of Hemingway's titles: *A Day's Wait*, *A Farewell to Arms*, and *A Moveable Feast*. I placed the books on the counter and handed the librarian my library card.

"Sorry," she said. "You have an outstanding book that either has to be returned or paid for before you can check out any more books."

"Really?" I said. "Which one?"

"Let's see. *Horton Hatches the Egg*. It's a Dr. Seuss book."

"I thought we returned it. I'll have to run home and get it."

"You know," continued the librarian, trying to be helpful, "if you'd just make a note on your calendar when your books are due and how many you need to return, you could avoid this type of situation."

"Thanks," I said weakly. "That *is* a good idea. I just didn't have time."

An hour later we exchanged Horton for Hemingway and headed home . . . again.

Because I didn't have ten minutes to plan my Sunday School lesson materials, I spent an hour on an unnecessary trip to the photocopier. Because I didn't have ten minutes to plan a week's menus, I wasted an hour on an unnecessary trip to the store. Because I didn't have thirty seconds to make a simple note on my calendar, I spent an hour retrieving a lost book. Just citing these three examples (I could recite three hundred more), twenty minutes of planning would have saved me three hours!

Gradually I began to realize the magnitude of this wasted time. I was affecting not only the quality of my own life, but that of my family as well. Every hour I wasted with needless activity was multiplied by the subliminal message I was passing on to our children: "Planning wastes time. There's no time to plan." It began a snowball effect. Their lack of planning compounded and increased the problems I was having with my own lack of planning. I stepped out of this vicious circle and realized there's no time *not* to plan.

Reason Number Three: Being organized is all right, but I prefer living.

Admittedly, the case for this reason was already pretty weak, based on the evidence presented in the aforementioned cases. However, I determined that I could not be an effective time manager, so I decided to compare well-managed days with days when I just more or less schlepped through life.

Interestingly, I discovered that on the days when I was on top of things I had higher self-esteem, more energy and ambition, a better disposition, and an overall feeling of well-being. Conversely, come-what-may days were more stress-laden, harried, and guilt-ridden, and fed a low self-image. I decided the living is better when it is nurtured in a positive, purposeful atmosphere. Oh sure, problems and crises still come along. No matter how organized, efficient, or effective we are, we never totally eliminate predicaments, though we may greatly reduce their frequency. Nevertheless, when trials do arise we're in better mental shape to handle them if we are on *top* of the heap instead of *under* it. Besides, the view is so much better from the summit.

Reason Number Four: It's not my fault.

If we were talking about heart problems here, reason number four would be the cholesterol conglomerate. This is the Big One. The Big Avocado. Here's where we go into high gear:

- I'm always interrupted.
- I can spend hours cleaning and in two minutes I have to start over.
- My husband is a slob.
- I don't have a husband.
- I'm waiting until things get back to normal.
- I just can't get organized around here.
- I work full-time.
- I'm bored. I need a job.
- My mother was disorganized.
- My mother was overly organized and I'm rebelling.
- I'm depressed.
- And on, and on, and on.

How do I know all this? Because I have a black belt in excuse-making. I have blamed my problems on kids, careers, and carpools; fate, fatigue, and female problems; men, messes, and money. You name it and I've pointed an accusing finger.

Just as I began to think I was on to something, I was pulled up short by a wise friend who said, "You know, Deniece, when you point one finger of blame, three other fingers are pointing directly back at you." While I was pondering that profound statement, the following incident occurred.

I was asked to conduct a seminar for a meeting planner and had an appointment at 1:30 P.M. to pick up the training materials. I was at the office promptly at 1:30 and was told I would have to wait because the training manuals were not ready yet. So I waited.

At 2:30 the manuals were boxed up and ready to go. "Jeff," I said to the person who was helping me, "if you'll carry this box out to my car, I'll carry the box with the handouts, the name cards, and the flip charts."

"Uh-oh," Jeff gasped. "Guess I forgot to get the handout packets ready. How many people are signed up for the class?"

"You tell me, Jeff. Didn't Susan give you the roll form?"

"Hey, Deniece, I'm really sorry about all this. Make yourself comfortable and I'll get my act together. This won't take long, I promise."

By approximately 3:00 P.M. the printed materials were ready and at last—or so I thought—I could be on my way. My hopes for departure were dashed, however, when Jeff said, "Don has the slide projector, screen, and tape recorder. Let me call his office and see if he'll put them in your car for you." Unfortunately, Don had the equipment in his car and had just left the office to make a bank deposit. "He should be back in a couple of minutes," Jeff assured me.

By 3:30 I finally pulled out of the parking lot, seething with anger. How could they waste two hours of my time? Those people were meeting planners. What a joke! I had better things to do with my time than sit around their office for two hours. From my point of view, the ubiquitous "they" were totally responsible for what I considered a vicious attack on my time.

After the heat of passion had passed, taking with it my self-righteous attitude, I had to admit to myself that *I* could have prevented the entire mishap. Perhaps they were to blame, but so was I. I could have called the office early in the day and reminded Jeff of our appointment. Together we could have run down the list of things I needed to pick up. I could have checked with Don and asked him to drop off the audiovisual materials in Jeff's office. I could also have called Susan to make sure the class roll was complete. All told, this would have taken five minutes and saved the better part of two hours.

Now, I wasn't totally converted to the "finger of blame" philosophy after only one incident, but slowly I have come to realize that I am not a powerless victim. I have more control—and thus more responsibility—over my life than I was willing to admit.

Reason Number Five: I don't have time.

I wanted to hone my piano skills, but I didn't have time to practice. I wanted to learn how to crochet, but I didn't have time to master a chain stitch. I wanted to read great biographies, but I didn't have time to choose one, let alone read it. About all I had time for was to make it through the day and keep my name out of the headlines.

Jim and I have been blessed with an abundance of wonderful friends who have had a great deal to do with my growth and development. One such friend was responsible for exposing reason number five as the myth it truly is. We were having dinner with Lowell and his wife, Nancy, and during the course of the evening Lowell noticed that I repeatedly used the phrase "I don't have time."

He said (and very kindly), "Deniece, you have time to do anything you want to do. It's just that you value another activity more than playing the piano, or learning how to crochet, or reading biographies." He continued, "So, every time you say 'I don't have time,' what you're really saying is 'I value something else more.' "

Now, whenever I catch myself saying "I don't have time," I stop dead in my tracks and say honestly, "I do have time, but I'm choosing to do something else."

Look over these five reasons and honestly admit that they are roadblocks to your progress:

1. I do not want to become a clock-watching robot.
2. Planning wastes time.
3. Being organized is all right, but I prefer living.
4. It's not my fault.
5. I don't have time.

You can learn from my experience to a limited degree, but you must begin gathering your own evidence to support the prosecution of these five excuses. Then and only then will you feel ownership of this time-management system, thus ensuring your success with it. When you discover something on your own, the impact of the experience lasts much longer than does the artificial high you feel by reading or hearing something inspiring or insightful. That's what I want for you. I want you to experience a permanent change in your life, not just a surge of motivation that will fade away in a few days.

Here is your assignment:

1. During the next few weeks, search for evidence to support my theories.

2. Think of a time when a few minutes of planning would have saved you a chunk of time.

3. At the end of a well-planned day, write down a few adjectives that describe your feelings.

4. Next time you're tempted to blame someone or something else, ask yourself, "What could I have done differently?"

5. Listen to yourself and notice how often you say, "I don't have time."

And, for heaven's sake, go clean out your handbag!

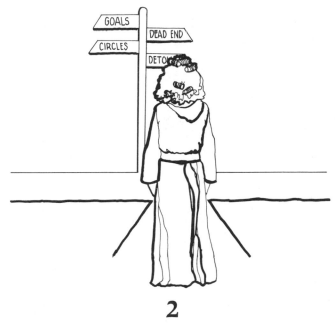

2

Direction Is More Important Than Speed

Take Time to Set Goals

A confession. For many years my personal approach to goal setting has been woefully riddled with questionable habits. First, I relied almost totally on one thing to get me going: fear. I would put off everything for as long as possible, from a high school homework assignment to mailing Christmas cards. The catalytic converter of my life was a roiling stomach and skin-prickling anxiety brought on by the advent of some unspeakable repercussion should I not meet the looming deadline.

Second, instead of simply planning steps for improvement I designed spectacular leaps:

- Read three books a week.
- Run five miles a day.

- Bake cookies every day before the kids get home from school.
- Become president of the company.
- Never take another bite of chocolate.
- Learn to like brussels sprouts.

Yes, I expected to soar with the eagles, but somehow I was always confined to ground level. You might say I pushed the self-destruct button too many times. However, I knew I was not a complete washout. I was reformable. And I also knew when to call for help.

Sir Isaac Newton once said, "If I have seen farther than other men, it is because I have stood on the shoulders of giants." I, too, stood on the shoulders of giants. I read. I studied. I interviewed. I investigated and came up with some character traits common to successful time managers:

1. They are always growing and learning. By setting and seeking after goals, we stay on a steady course of growth and intellectual development.

2. They are organized. Planning the specific course to follow helps us organize our efforts and provides us with the shortest route between where we are now and where we want to go.

3. Their lives are balanced. We can keep our lives in balance by setting goals in four life-encompassing categories: intellectual, physical, spiritual, and social.

4. They are self-disciplined. As we strive to pursue our chosen course, we exercise the powers of self-mastery and strengthen our ability to discipline ourselves.

Finally, my maturity and intelligence melded to the point where I realized that to meet the criteria for being a successful time manager, I had to plan goals and plan them correctly.

I, like you, have read all the jargon about planning goals. I'm sure you're familiar with the terms long-range, intermediate, and short-term goals. What I'm going to show you, though, is a refreshing change: simple goal setting for complicated people.

But first, why plan goals? What do goals have to do with time management? Plenty. What you do today is what you are tomorrow. And, if you are what you eat, then certainly you become what you do! Here's a poignant example taken from the May 6, 1985, issue of *Time*.

"Sentenced: Dennis Dale (Denny) McLain, 41, Detroit Tigers pitching star from 1963 to 1970, whose 31-6 record in 1968 makes him the last pitcher in the major leagues to post a 30-win season; to 23 years in prison, including 3 concurrent 8-year terms for racketeering, extortion, and conspiracy and 15 years for possession of 3 kg. of cocaine with intent to sell; in Tampa, Fla. Said a tearful McLain: 'I don't know how you get to where I am today from where I was 17 years ago.' "

We get off course because we don't look at our goals—what we truly want out of life—every single day and ask ourselves, "What can I do *today* to bring my goals closer to fruition? Are the things I've planned to do today in keeping with the goals I've set for myself?" Yes, time management is life management, and a life can be managed only if worthy goals are set and strived for.

Before I explain my simple goal-setting system, I want you to shrink your rearview mirror. Your what? Your rearview mirror.

Because drivers need to maintain perspective and know what is approaching from the rear, a small mirror is attached to the windshield of the car. Though it is much smaller than the windshield, without it we could easily be run over by a cement mixer. The mirror (or a rubber neck) is essential for safe driving.

But suppose the rearview mirror was almost as large as the windshield. We'd have little chance of arriving at our destination with our appendages intact. The mirror would obstruct our view of the road and the approaching reality that must be encountered.

How does this relate to goals? You must not dwell on your past goal-setting failures. Shrink that mirror so you can still see them and be taught by them, but don't let setbacks halt your progress.

In January 1985 I compiled a prioritized list of books I wanted to read during the year. There were fifteen titles on that list and I read only ten of them. Actually, I did not reach my goal, did I? But I did read ten books trying to get there.

My point is that when you strive toward a goal, you achieve more than if you hadn't tried at all, even if you don't quite make it. So, set goals, work for them, and start over when you get stuck. But don't let that old rearview mirror come between you and the windshield.

One more note before we get started with the goal-planning activity. While it is important to work toward goals as a family, for our purposes here I would like to concentrate on personal goal development. Ultimately, the only person you can control is YOU. When you involve others in a goal, you can use leadership skills to encourage and influence, but you cannot completely control the results. For now, we'll take the attitude, "Let it begin with me." Besides, *improvement*, as you know, begins with I.

OK. Take a piece of paper and divide it into four columns (or use four separate sheets of paper), one for each of the following goal categories: intellectual, physical, spiritual, and social. My goal in teaching this goal-setting system is that after you've finished reading this book, you'll sit down and formulate one goal in each of these categories.

Following are examples of the types of activities involved in each area of focus:

Intellectual

- Developing or enlarging a talent
- Cultural development
- Reading good literature
- Career development
- Education development
- Financial security

Physical

- Weight guidelines
- Athletic skills
- Exercise program
- Health and nutrition
- Grooming
- Medical and dental care
- Occupational and/or homemaking skills

Social

- Any type of charitable service
- Improving social skills

Spiritual

- Journal keeping
- Church service
- Character development
- Family life

Don't spend a lot of time deciding which category a goal belongs in. The only reason for the divisions in the first place is to make sure certain areas of your life are not being neglected, while others are tipping the scale.

In addition to the above ideas, here are some questions to help galvanize your thoughts:

- What bothers me most about my life right now? (Do not blame others for your station in life. Concentrate only on what *you* can do to change things.)
- Can I make any changes that will make me more successful or happy? If so, what are they?
- I could function more effectively if . . . ?
- What do I enjoy doing?
- What does my conscience tell me I should be doing? (Remember, your conscience is not solely to scold, but to encourage you to do better.)

Ask yourself these questions in each frame of reference, jotting down everything that comes to mind. Right now, you're just brainstorming. As soon as you're satisfied with your list, you can start the selection process.

To begin with, choose only one goal from each category. If you overprogram yourself, you just might overload the circuit, blow a fuse, and burn out before you even get started. Remember for now, at least, that direction is more important than speed.

Once you've singled out a goal in each category, write it down. There is something physiologically and psychologically connected with writing the goal. Somehow you're more committed to a goal that's specified on paper.

Many years ago a weary traveler entered the town where Mark Twain had lived as a young man. Encountering an old man who had been a citizen of the community for many years, the traveler asked, "Did you know Mark Twain?" "Sure did," replied the old man. "Knew just as many stories as he did, too. Only difference is, he writ 'em down."

Yes, Mark Twain "writ 'em down" all right, and that's why the world knows *his* name instead of the name of his neighbor.

Write the goal down. Now take a look at it and be sure you've written the goal and not just a way to achieve it. For example: "Run five miles a day" is probably not a goal but a goal activity. Most likely the goal is: "Become physically fit so as to improve my physical stamina, health, appearance, and mental well-being." Running five miles a day is one way to meet this goal. In addition, other goal activities might be: have a physical examination by the doctor; reduce my intake of fats, sodium, and cholesterol; drink eight glasses of water every day; and so on.

To measure your progress and chart the results, write the goal as specifically as possible. For example, the physical fitness goal mentioned above is acceptable but this is better: "I want to be physically fit. I will have reached that goal when

I weigh 125 pounds with body fat not to exceed 20 percent." Now, that's specific!

Here's the easy part. Every time you plan a goal, don't worry too much about the techniques of goal writing. Just answer these effective goal-directing questions:

- What am I going to do?
- How am I going to do it?
- When am I going to do it?
- Where can I do it?
- Who (or what) can help me?
- Why am I going to do this?
- When do I expect to complete my goal?

Let's see this list in action, using the physical fitness goal stated previously.

1. *What am I going to do?* I am going to become physically fit. My weight will be 125 pounds and my body fat will not exceed 20 percent.

2. *How am I going to do it?* I will begin a jogging program, working slowly and gradually up to a thirty-minute run. During bad weather I will use an aerobic videotape (working up to thirty minutes). I will also limit my intake of fats and sugar.

3. *When am I going to do it?* I will do it every day until I reach my goal, then three times a week to maintain. I will work out when the children get home from school.

4. *Where can I do it?* I will jog at the high school track, on the street in front of our house, at home in the family room when I use the VCR.

5. *Who (or what) can help me?* I will read a few books about physical fitness. The two older children can also help me by taking turns watching the baby during my exercise sessions.

6. *Why am I going to do this?* I want to increase my energy level and help fight fatigue, to improve my appearance, to boost my self-esteem.

7. When do I expect to complete my goal? I will reach 125 pounds six months from today, though it may take two years for the body fat level to drop to 20 percent.

Once these questions are answered, you can be sure that your goal has been well stated and outlined. It may help you to monitor your progress if you capsulize the goal activities onto one list such as this:

- Walk daily, working up to thirty minutes jogging.
- Get the books *Fit or Fat* and *How to Lower Your Fat Thermostat* and read three chapters a day until both books are completed.
- Arrange for the older children to babysit while I work out.
- Eliminate candy, soda pop, ice cream, and deep-fried foods from my diet (at least during weekdays).

Then finish the list with the date you will start and the expected completion date.

Record keeping is an important part of setting and achieving your goals. It encourages your development and deepens your sense of commitment. Progress is easier when you work with a written plan and timetable, making frequent checkups along the way to measure your growth. Also, you can compare yourself in relationship to your own past performances as opposed to the feats of others. You can get ahead of yourself and concentrate on breaking your own records, working harder than you have ever done before to achieve new heights.

If you feel overwhelmed, if you think there's no time to work on your goals right now, think again. Write down your goals. They will give you a reason to get out of bed in the morning. You'll be able to choose what to do and what not to do, feel less overwhelmed, and have greater control. You'll be able to put your priorities in order. In short, you'll enjoy enormous peace of mind and a tremendous boost to your self-image.

Years ago I worked as a secretary in downtown Chicago. Going to work every morning and coming home every night, I was caught in bumper-to-bumper rush-hour traffic. I traveled on the Dan Ryan Expressway, which was sometimes hailed as the world's largest parking lot, and twice a day I was witness to that fact. Day after day I sat in that knot of traffic, sometimes making progress only inches at a time. But day after day I did arrive at work, and day after day I did get back home. The pace didn't matter—the goal did!

On August 5, 1984, the famed Welsh actor Richard Burton died of a cerebral hemorrhage. The day following his death a newspaper headline read "Richard Burton: A Genius Who Squandered His Greatness."

As I read that headline, I asked myself, "Am I squandering my greatness? Am I living up to my potential? Am I doing everything I possibly can to make the most out of my life?" Of course, in a moment of self-honesty I had to answer, "No. But I'm doing a lot better than I was ten years ago." Direction is more important than speed.

There are really no instant winners, but there are constant winners. Your goals can be met even if you take slow, predetermined steps. Even a slow, steady stream of water will in time erode the hardest rock. Don't wait for the perfect situation to set some goals. Do it now!

3

Your Declaration of Dependence

Make a Planning Notebook

Planning notebooks are my version of chicken soup. If used correctly, they will cure any time-management malady you suffer from.

Perhaps you're already a list maker. Before I started using a planning notebook I was a list maker too, but I made lists the way some people take two aspirins and lie down for a while. My lists provided only temporary relief of anxiety and were rarely consulted again. Not that I could have consulted them if I'd wanted to. My list-making system was decidedly decentralized what with scribbles on paper towels, envelopes, kitchen counters, and wooden studs in the basement. Calendars, I thought, were only for dates, deadlines, and appointments, and as a full-time homemaker I had few, if any, dates, deadlines, or appointments.

"Why should I lug this thing around?" I'd say. "I can certainly remember the dentist appointment next week. Besides, the secretary will probably call and remind me anyway." So, I tossed the calendar in the garbage and went on my merry way grabbing scratch paper, cereal boxes, paper plates, and telephone books—not to mention the half-inch border around the newspaper. More lengthy reminders were scrawled on yellow legal pads.

An envelope from some cast-off junk mail seemed like a good place for a grocery list. And when I needed to jot down directions to get somewhere, the cardboard backing from my purse packet of Kleenex served the purpose quite nicely. *Who needs calendars?* I thought.

As my life got busier and my addled brain more absent-minded, I decided to give calendars one last try. With the fervor of an archaeological dig, I tried every calendaring system known to the free world. I finally got wise to the fact that a calendar you can personalize seems to work the best.

Here's where the nitty gets gritty. In the course of the next three chapters I will outline a winning time-management system in detail, and all you'll have to do are three things:

1. Set up a planning notebook.
2. Set up a family organizer.
3. Control your environment.

The first two steps are one-shot deals. Once you set them up, all you have to do is use them. Admittedly, step number three is slightly harder and is an ongoing process, but in chapter 5, I'll give you lots of helpful time-management tips and tricks so your resolve won't dissolve before you begin to get a taste of success.

Do you want to be a time-management winner? If you want to successfully manage your home, nurture your family, and still have the time and energy left for personal development, then the answer is yes, you do want to be a time-management winner—and you will be, if you apply the principles in this book step by step. So here we go with step number one.

What is a planning notebook? First, it's a calendar, and second, it's a personalized directory of information you need to refer to on a regular and ongoing basis. It contains dates, deadlines, and appointments, but also lots of other information that comes to you. Basically, a planning notebook holds anything you want it to.

Where can you get one? There is certainly no shortage of calendars on the market. If you take a swing through your local bookstore or the stationery section of your favorite department store, you'll discover a wide array of calendars, miscellaneous forms, and planning pages.

The calendar I use is the least complex system I've found. It combines month at a glance with one page per day calendar formats. That way, I can see my whole month, yet still have room for daily plans and reminders. For information, just write to me at PO Box 214, Cedar Rapids, Iowa 52406.

What should you look for when you buy a calendar?

1. Be sure the calendar is big enough to record everything you need to keep track of and small enough to be portable. I've used the 5½" x 8" size for years and found it to be the most convenient for me.

2. Check the calendar format and determine if it provides a good structure for you. For a long time I used the week-at-a-glance set-up. Once when I was demonstrating it, a woman raised her hand and said, "I have panic attacks if I see more than one date at a time." For people like her, there are day-at-a-glance designs. Actually, there are so many different formats, you may want to experiment a little until you feel comfortable with one.

3. If the system you're considering is so complicated that you need to read a set of instructions before using it, don't buy it. There's no reason to make your life more complicated. Simplicity is the solution to most of life's problems.

4. Flip through the entire calendar before you buy it, to see if there is a lot of material in it that you don't want. For example, years ago I had a beautiful calendar that contained articles (yes, articles) with such titles as "Sand, Sun, and Serenity," "Bronze Age Ships," and "Hideaways from Headlines," to name only a few. Also in this volume were various tidbits of information: how many inches of rain fell in Des Moines, Iowa, in 1981, the recommended thickness of household insulation (it's six inches, in case you're wondering), and how to locate the solenoid in your car. So, look over the calendar before you buy it. There's no sense paying for something you can't use.

5. Because of the personalized aspect of the planning notebook, I recommend a looseleaf binder so you can add, even temporarily, any information you want to include. Some brands of looseleaf calendars come with tabbed dividers and blank pages so you can personalize the sections. Sometimes, however, these must be purchased separately at an office supply store.

6. Be sure the book is attractive. Why? If it's on the shabby side, you'll leave it on the front seat of the car, on the kitchen counter, in the diaper bag, or on your desk at the

office. If it's handsome, you'll want to use it and carry it with you everywhere. And that's when it really becomes functional—when it's hermetically sealed to your right hand.

Once I was speaking to a women's organization and I noticed several of the ladies were carrying calendars with mink covers. While I'm not advocating that you hock your jewelry or take out a second mortgage to get a mink calendar, I think these women had the right idea.

Once you purchase the looseleaf calendar, how do you set up the rest of the book? I think it's best to let the personalized sections in the planning notebook evolve naturally. Here's what I mean.

While I was developing my calendaring habit, I was at the same time collecting a potpourri of motivational thoughts and quotes, words that made me laugh or spurred me on to better action. I kept this assemblage in a small notebook and carried it in my purse. It was always with me so that wherever I was and whenever I heard or read another irresistible tidbit, I could include it in the collection. Mark Twain often said that you should always have two books with you—one to write in and one to read. The calendar and my book of thoughts filled his requirements.

My pilot light was not exactly on "low" but my rheostat was definitely on "dim." Then, as if someone had grabbed the control and illuminated the darkness, I realized I could simplify things if I were to combine the calendar and the thoughts into one book. I soon found that one reinforced the other. I began to keep a to-do list on the daily calendar pages, listing housecleaning chores, errands, and phone calls to make. The book of thoughts was in my hands more often than before, and I could memorize some of the more noteworthy quotations.

One afternoon while driving around town, I impulsively decided to stop at the library before going home. I had been looking for a particular book and wanted to see if it was available at our local branch. As I flipped through the card catalog and discovered the book wasn't registered, I suddenly wished for a book list I had kept carefully filed away in my office. I was in a mood to read but couldn't remember the titles of the books I had on my to-read list. So, disappointed and empty-handed, I journeyed home, but the rheostat circled full force once again. As soon as I walked into the house, I included my book list behind a tabbed divider, and my planning notebook was born. By degrees it evolved into a single source for organizing and planning my life. It is a means whereby I can accomplish more of the things I should do and fewer of the things that don't matter in the long run.

So, why do *you* need one? Whether you realize it or not, you are at the highest level of management without a secretary. There's no one to screen your calls, no one to make your appointments and remind you of them, no one to hand you the mail in priority order, and no one to intercept interruptions. It's just you against time with no buffer to offer protection from its ravages. And ravages they are! For every day we are faced with a complicated melange of

> Piano lessons, dental sessions,
> Trips to Pittsburgh, Timbuktu,
> Filing, mending, baby tending,
> Books to read and goals to do;
> Birthday present, stuff a pheasant,
> Turn the clocks back, note the dates,
> Journal keeping, kitchen sweeping,
> Wash a stack of dirty plates;
> Exercising, organizing,
> Take the Cub Scouts to the zoo,
> Calls to make, notes to take,
> Writing a report or two,
> Mail to read and kids to feed,
> Clipping coupons, things for free;
> Budget chopping, grocery shopping,
> Lights strung on the Christmas tree!

One of the hardest facts about life is that by the time you're one-third of the way through, you realize it's strictly a do-it-yourself job. All the more reason for a planning note-book. The planning notebook I use has many sections, each behind a labeled, tabbed divider. This is where the system can work for you, too. Pick and choose to include in your notebook whatever it is that *you* need to know to keep you headed in the desired direction. To give you some ideas, here's what I include (or have included from time to time) in my planning notebook.

The first section is the calendar section. How I use this section will be explained in chapter 5.

Inserted after the calendar section is a running to-do list. These are jobs I know I must do sometime but I'm not sure when. Since I can't assign these chores to a specific date, I use this running to-do list as a place holder. Every day when I work up my daily to-do's, I check the running to-do section for tasks to include on today's list. (This process will also be explained further in chapter 5.)

Next comes a section of goals I'm working on. In this category are personal goals, a list of craft projects I've cho-sen to work on during the year, and a list of things that would be nice to do someday (these are potential goals, though they're still in the incubator). A dear friend is always pre-senting me with handmade gifts. Someday I'd like to make something for her. The nice-to-do list holds some ideas, such as that snow family in the December 1984 issue of *Christmas Crochet Collection*, which would be fun to make for a Christ-mas decoration. The nice-to-do list reminds me of an idea and tells me where to find it again.

Now, if I never did these things, nothing drastic would happen, but the list gives me a selection of ideas to choose from plus the security of knowing I won't forget a good inten-tion.

I also keep in the goals section two other lists: five-minute tasks and rewards.

By itemizing things I can accomplish in five minutes I'm not implying that any of us should be busy, busy, busy every waking minute of the day. Doing absolutely nothing is great as long as we don't do it all the time. The reason I've included this chart in my planning notebook is because of my personality. I tend to be the kind of person who waits for ideal moments. (When I have a whole day with nothing to do, I'll clean the basement. When Schuyler finally goes to college, I'll catch up the baby books. We're not going to hang a job chart in our house until I can do one in cross-stitch.) My five-minute task list is there to gently remind me that no one has enough time to use only ideal moments. Don't let an imperfect situation be an excuse to do nothing.

The reward list is a lot of fun. Here's how it works. Whenever I feel a surge of excitement or motivation, I note the cause on my reward list: read, buy a plant, go out for a cheese enchilada, bake a cake, rummage through a second-hand store, crochet, catch up on filing. My reward list is quite long by now, and whenever I need to get myself up and going, I can always find something on that list that excites me. For example, the real motivation for finishing this manuscript is that as soon as it's completed I can start making afghans for our children's birthdays this year. I'm so excited about that project that my pen just glides across the paper.

I know what you're thinking: "How could 'catch up on filing' be a reward?" While some would consider that an onerous burden, I enjoy doing it—though the mood usually hits only semiannually. The purpose of a reward list is to run the gamut of my emotions. What interests me one day might not even be tempting the next. But there's always at least one thing on the list that gets my heart pumping.

I believe that the only psychological theory that has withstood the test of time is "behavior persists when it is rewarded." Formulate a reward list and start rewarding yourself. When you need some inspiration to complete a distasteful job, just have one of those rewards waiting—and watch your performance soar.

Menu-selection sheets are contained in another section in my notebook. These pages remind me of all the dishes we like to have for dinner. An ingredients list for each dish is also included. This section is a good place for recording inventory in the freezer, food storage, or pantry.

Armed with all this information, I'm never caught off guard when I go shopping. "This is a good sale on chicken. I wonder how many chickens I still have in the freezer?" My inventory sheets give me the answer.

The menu-selection sheets help me plan menus quickly; and with the ingredients list and inventories so handy, it is simple (and fast) to shop the ads, use coupons and leftovers, and take advantage of in-store specials.

Next up is the purchase section. This is where I list things I'd like to buy someday when I have some extra money. I jot down things that would make life just a little easier, such as a towel rack for the kitchen, a tote for the minicassette recorder, a drawer divider for the silverware, a trash basket for Brian's bedroom. There are some real advantages to having a section such as this. First of all, when I list a desired item, my desire begins to age. Sometimes my enthusiasm for a particular object will wane, and sometimes it dies a natural death. ("I don't want one anymore." "I know someone who has one and they never use it.")

So I jot things on my list and see if they will stand the test of time, before I make a purchase. I may save some money. On the other hand, sometimes having a wanted item written down serves as an impetus to budget and save for it.

I suppose my favorite reason for having a purchase section is secondhand stores. Here's why: Our home has been decorated with things purchased at various outlets. I list certain things I'm looking for, check the shops regularly, and pretty soon they show up. I've saved a fortune, and it's a fun hobby. I get the excitement of spending money coupled with the thrill of getting a bargain—and all for a worthy cause. I've bought baskets (our house is full of them), drawer dividers, bins, furniture, books, and my wonderful fifteen-dollar IBM electric typewriter! Yes, the purchase section is essential.

Are you beginning to see why calendars alone are not sufficient? Can you see how much time you can save with a planning notebook?

The most used and versatile section in my planner is the special-data section. (That's just a fancy way of saying *miscellaneous*.) This is where I keep birthday and anniversary lists, clothing sizes for family members, battery numbers (for watches, cameras, calculators, toys, and so forth), number of the slide-projector bulb, size of the furnace filter and evaporative cooler pads, shoelace lengths, sock and shoe sizes, kids' locker numbers and combinations, school schedules, prescription numbers, telephone area codes and time zones—and my to-purchase list.

A holiday section can keep you celebrating if you observe holidays in a big way. Whenever you see an attractive decorating idea, read a delicious-sounding holiday recipe, or hear about a clever tradition, write it down in the holiday section. If you've seen a craft pattern for something you'd like to make, note where you saw the directions. This is also a good place to list supplies left over from the previous holiday; then, when the holiday rolls around again, you won't have to remember what's being stored and you'll be able to purchase accurately.

Here are some more section ideas:

- A section to record summer activity ideas for the kids.
- A temporary section for to-do's and information for an upcoming wedding, departure for college, or plans for a reunion dinner you're in charge of.
- A family section with sizes, measurements, and ideas for gifts.
- Sections for financial matters, insurance, journal entries, personal data, immunization records, decorating ideas (include the colors of your rooms and measurements for windows, beds, and rooms), addresses, and telephone numbers.

There. That ought to give you a pretty good start. One question I'm often asked is if I take my planning notebook everywhere. Yes, I do. Of course, I don't pack it into a nice restaurant when Jim and I go out to dinner on Saturday night, and I wouldn't take it to the symphony or to the movies, but you can be sure it's in the car, at least. (I'll admit I get very nervous when it's not close by.) And on those few occasions when the planner is not in my hands, I have a pen and a few index cards in my purse on which to record pertinent information, ideas, and plans. These notes are then transferred to the planning notebook during my next daily planning session.

Now, to summarize, as you read this book, think of ways to personalize *your* planning notebook. What sections would you include? Remember that the four most important sections are calendar, running to-do list, goals, and special data. The planning notebook works in tandem with the family organizer, which we'll discuss in the next chapter. Then, with those two tools in order, you'll see how the management system actually works.

So what's in it for you? Here's when you hit pay dirt and receive the real payoff: more time for you!

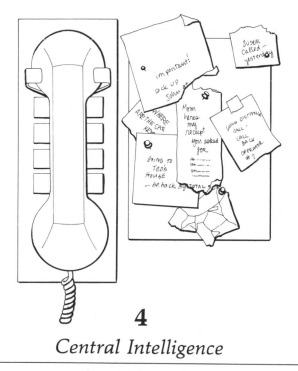

4

Central Intelligence

Make a Family Organizer

If your children can't find anything but the wall, the kitchen counter, or the front of a coloring book to write phone messages on; if your refrigerator is covered with magnetized notes and reminders; if you find it difficult remembering the time of the next dance recital and whose turn it is to do the dishes—this chapter is for you.

Follow my suggestions and you'll never have to scribble notes and phone numbers on the backs of envelopes, business cards, matchbooks, grocery sacks, or check-deposit slips. You won't be plagued by those omnipresent scraps of floating paper. What's more, you'll be able to locate desired information with blinding speed. No, no, you don't need an Apple II. All it takes is a family organizer.

What is that? It's a three-ring binder (ours is a full-sized 8½ x 11 inches) that holds everything from telephone logs to football game schedules. For added convenience we have one upstairs and a duplicate downstairs.

The beauty of the system is that it holds anything *you* want it to hold, though it should contain everything you search for on a regular basis. Then it becomes a central information center for the whole family.

To make a family organizer, you will need a three-ring binder, tabbed dividers, telephone logs, and planning sheets for the kids (optional). Here is a list of sections to consider including in your family organizer:

1. *Telephone Logs.* Telephone logs were born out of dire necessity. If writing miscellaneous phone numbers and notes on tiny scraps of paper were a sign of Chinese nobility, my dear husband would be the head of the Ming Dynasty, at least. He'll come home with a napkin shoved inside his pocket, retrieve it carefully, and toss it in one of the drawers in the kitchen. Sixty days—and as many or more notes—later, he'll say, "Hey, where is Ed's phone number? It was on a piece of a blue napkin that I put in this drawer last April." Well, who knows where Ed's phone number is, or the message Jim got from Marty's Motor Salvage, or the Bug Busters new address, or a hundred other pieces of trivia. With my nose only inches above the paper line, I called a halt to the papernoia and introduced the family to telephone logs.

As you can see by the illustration on page 41, this is a sheet of 8½ x 11-inch paper that's divided into five vertical columns headed by date, message for, caller, phone number, message. The page is then ruled horizontally every one-half inch (or triple spaced on the typewriter).

I made up a master telephone log and photocopied a stack of them. Then I placed several behind a tabbed and labeled divider in the family organizer. When one sheet is completely filled in and all the messages are taken care of, we remove it from the book and put it with other completed pages. (Ours

TELEPHONE LOG

Month _____

Date	Message for	Caller	Phone Number	Message

are clamped together with a large paper clamp and hung inside a cupboard door.)

Now, if we need a long-lost number, we can flip through the completed phone logs and quickly discover it. However, if you refer frequently to old phone logs to find a certain phone number, that number should be recorded in a more permanent place. We usually discard the old logs after they're six months old.

These logs have some obvious advantages: (1) When a child is taking a message, the columns remind him what information needs to be recorded. (2) All calls and phone numbers become a permanent record. (3) The logs become a complete message center. For example, one message written to me from Jeff, our ten-year-old, tells me he went to Barrett's house. (4) You eliminate floating scraps of paper and hours of wasted time.

Even if you make up only one family organizer, it is extremely beneficial to keep at least one telephone log near each phone.

Occasionally we've run out of telephone log sheets and had to rely on the old scratch-pad method until I've had a chance to have more forms printed. Those times of temporary inconvenience further serve to remind me of the value of the telephone logs. Once you've started using them, you will be totally convinced of their effectiveness.

2. *Emergency Phone Numbers.* Here you include your name, address, and phone number. (During a crisis or emergency, your children or the babysitter may not remember your address or phone number, so it's important to include this information.) Also list numbers for ambulance, fire, paramedics, police, family doctor, hospital, and poison-control center. This section is a good place for the names, addresses, and phone numbers of the next-door neighbors and next of kin. Some families also include a signed medical-release form.

3. *Phone Directory.* This is simply a listing of frequently called phone numbers, such as schools, libraries, favorite stores and restaurants, theaters, the children's friends, and our

friends. Whenever you catch yourself looking up the same phone numbers over and over, put them in this section.

These three sections—telephone logs, emergency phone numbers, and the phone directory—are mandatory if you want your family organizer to be most effective.

In addition, here are some optional, yet extremely useful, ideas to consider:

1. *Weekly Planning Sheets.* As you'll notice in the illustration on page 44, these are 8½ x 11-inch pages divided into seven horizontal columns (one for each day of the week) and four vertical columns: assignments, chores, activities and appointments, and things I want to do. Every Sunday afternoon, I sit down with my children and fill in the planning sheets (one for each child) and place them in the family organizer. Then I remove the previous week's sheets and have the children write a weekly journal entry on the back. These sheets are placed in separate binders for safekeeping. This is a highly effective way of formulating a child's life history.

2. *Household.* This section could contain your housekeeping schedule, a master list of where stored items are kept, inventory sheets from the freezer and food storage, a metric conversion table, a record of weights and equivalents, household hints, and the family schedule items. (For example: the milkman comes Monday, Wednesday, and Friday. Matt and Jim take piano on Tuesday at 4:30 and 5:00 P.M. Hospital volunteer work is done the first Tuesday of every month. PTA meeting is the fourth Thursday of every month. Aerobics class is every Wednesday at 10:00 A.M., and so on.)

Should someone come home and need to locate you, this schedule might give a clue as to your whereabouts. Also, if for some unexpected reason, someone has to come in and take over your family, they will be well aware of your household routine.

3. *Facts for the Babysitter.* Here you list the baby's schedule, naptimes, bedtimes, family rules (no playing outside after dinner; 10-minute phone limit; list of accepted TV shows;

WEEKLY PLANNING SHEET

Name _____

	Chores	Assignments	Activities & Appointments	I Want to Do
MONDAY				
TUESDAY				
WEDNESDAY				
THURSDAY				
FRIDAY				
SATURDAY				
SUNDAY				

snacking privileges, and so on). Actually, the other sections of the family organizer are helpful to the sitter too.

4. *Sports.* With a resident coach and five budding athletes in our family, I soon learned the meaning of the term "the paper explosion." After the first practice (be it soccer, baseball, basketball, football, hockey, Ping-Pong, dance, or whatever), each person brings home at least four pieces of paper: team roster, practice schedule, game schedule, and game locations.

And on game day what usually happens? You can't find the right paper so you call another kid who's also on the team and get the rundown from *his* mom. Just ask my neighbor Kristy Jenkins. Every time her phone rings during baseball season, she picks up the receiver and, without even saying "Hello," says, "Hi, Deniece." Kristy was about to switch over to a taped recording when (and she was relieved to hear this) I started putting the sports information into our family organizer.

Using this system, everyone can quickly check dates and verify times, though I do get lonely for Kristy's cheerful voice.

5. *Membership Directories.* When I receive a membership directory from our church or from other organizations to which we belong, I include those directories in the family organizer if they'll be referred to often and if they're compact and not too bulky. (Large directories are stored with the telephone books.)

If your family organizer has a pocket inside the front cover, that's a good spot for smaller pamphlet-sized directories or information booklets.

Family organizer rules to live by:

1. Have one family organizer on each floor of your home.

2. Put telephone logs and pencils by the remaining phones.

3. Duplicate all information (sports rosters, emergency information, directories, and so on) for each family organizer. (Note: I do not duplicate the kids' planning sheets.

Those are included only in the kitchen copy. Information booklets, such as the ones sent home on the first day of school, are also found only in the kitchen family organizer.)

4. Coordinate the directory sections at least once every six months or so. For example, you note Diane's new phone number in the downstairs family organizer. The number should also be placed in the upstairs copy to keep both directories current. This will also keep you from running downstairs every time you want to call Diane.

I've given phone logs to thousands of people and have received as many testimonials of their value. However, I've heard a few excuses too. Here's the most common: "Now, when I come home from work, I'll have to go to every phone to get my messages."

Think about it. Wouldn't you have to do that anyway? If your sixteen-year-old answers the phone in his bedroom and takes a message for you, does he run into the kitchen and post it on the bulletin board or on the front of the refrigerator so you'll be sure to see it? (If he does, I'll trade you sixteen-year-olds.) We've found that most of our phone messages are fielded in the kitchen, so the bulk of the activity is with that family organizer.

These are just a few ideas to get you going. Personalize your book just as we did with a planning notebook. How about a section for birthdays and anniversaries, family records, monthly expenses? It's only limited by your imagination. Just remember that the family organizer contains information you need to refer to at home. It is used and referred to by the whole family. On the other hand, the planning notebook contains things you personally need to have with you when you're away from home as well.

Before we started using our family organizer, I had to find places for all these things: phone messages, organizational directories, rosters, schedules, and emergency phone numbers. Now everything is housed in one compact unit. Sometimes I wonder how we ever managed without it!

As you can see, the family organizer eliminates so much clutter and confusion and saves so much time, it's a must for every home. If you're still not convinced, just try it for one month. I'm positive you'll become a convert, spreading the word with missionary zeal.

5

Use Your Head to Save Your Heels

How the System Works

Years ago as we were walking through the exhibits at the Utah State Fair, we came across a booth displaying knitted baby clothes. Being a knitter myself and seeming to always be in the market for baby clothes, I became the perfect customer. As I oohed and ahhed over each outfit, I couldn't help noticing a woman whom I perceived to be a gypsy. She was feverishly pulling one set of clothes after another off the racks.

My suspicions were raised, I suppose, by her rather bohemian appearance. Her billowing blouse, awash with color, hung loosely about her shoulders and contrasted sharply with her long, flowing calico skirt. Her dark hair was knotted under a red cotton kerchief; and beneath the folds of the scarf, one silver dangling earring caressed her right jaw.

But it was what she said more than how she looked that convinced me she was, indeed, a gypsy. As she gathered her selected bundle of clothes and made her way to the proprietor she said in broken English but with an air of authority, "If you will give me these clothes for free, I will tell your fortune."

Slightly embarrassed and somewhat at a loss for words, the young woman who owned the shop said faintly, "Oh, well, I guess you'll have to talk to my husband." (Husbands are great, aren't they? You can get out of so many things if you have one!)

Scouting around, the gypsy soon found the young woman's husband and repeated her offer. "If you will give me these clothes for free, I will tell your fortune."

"No, ma'am," the man said politely. "I don't think so."

However, the woman would not be vanquished. Finally, in order to silence her harping, the businessman said, "It is my belief that we each tell our own fortunes by the things we choose to do every day."

I have thought of that incident many times, and though that shop owner was young in years, he was certainly old in wisdom. I believe, as well, that we tell our own fortunes.

But how do you choose what things to do today when so many things seem to be equally important? And how do you get onto the more important things when daily acts of maintenance eat up every available minute of your time?

If you are running a little late, here is what has happened so far, in brief. During the two preceding chapters we discussed how to set up a planning notebook and a family organizer. Now it's time to see how the system works and how it will answer those pressing questions while keeping you from ever running late again!

For over a decade, I used a planning notebook and enjoyed a great measure of success with it. Every day in the calendar section I recorded upcoming dates, deadlines, appointments, and a list of things to do each day—a daily action plan. And when I thought of things I had to do but didn't know when I was going to do them, I listed those tasks in the running to-do section. Consulted on a daily basis, this section fed my daily action plan. Every day I'd take one or two things off the to-do list and add them to my daily action plan.

But it wasn't until I met Dr. Hobbs that I learned I was not using my calendar section to its full potential. He taught me that not only should dates, deadlines, appointments, and a to-do list be recorded, but all information that comes to me can be and should be recorded in the calendar section of the planning notebook. Here are some examples of what I mean:

1. You receive a wedding invitation in the mail. Let's pretend the wedding is on February 7. Flip ahead in your calendar to February 7 and record all pertinent information: the time and place of the wedding, and the time and place of the reception, and so on. Now flip to the running to-do section and add this item to the list: "Purchase wedding gift for Steve and Sally before February 7." Then throw the invitation away.

2. The Gastronomical Gourmet is whipping up Potatoes Good-Woman Style on TV. The recipe sounds delicious, nutritious, and fast, and you just *have* to add it to your repertoire. Instead of reaching for the back of an envelope, a corrected spelling test, or a magazine cover, or running to the kitchen for a recipe card, you grab your planning notebook (which is always close by, of course) and open it to today's date. Record the recipe and then flip to the running to-do section and add this to the list: "Try Potatoes Good-Woman Style (Jan. 15)." The numbers in the parentheses are today's date, telling you that the recipe can be found on the January 15 calendar page.

3. One spring afternoon, your son comes home from school with a sheet telling you about baseball sign-ups. Let's say sign-ups will be held every Saturday in April at the Community Center from 10:00 A.M. to 2:00 P.M. The cost is $35.00. You need to bring a medical insurance policy number and a doctor's completed physical examination form when the child is registered. Once again, open your calendar to today's date and briefly write down all the information. Turn to your

running to-do section and add this to the growing list: "Baseball sign-ups in April on Saturdays (Mar. 18)." Remember, Mar. 18 is the date where the information about baseball sign-ups is recorded in your calendar. Then throw away the original paper, the one your son brought home.

4. You're on a lunch break and everyone is buzzing about a new Thai restaurant that opened up last weekend. You love Thai food and want to record all the details. What do you do? Reach for a "While You Were Out Today" pad? No. Open your planning notebook to today's date and jot the name and address of the restaurant and anything else you learn, such as price range, business hours, and party accommodations. Then in the running to-do section you write, "Try Thai Foon Restaurant (April 17)."

Now, don't argue. I can feel your resistance. You're wondering why you should record that information about the wedding or the baseball sign-ups. Wouldn't it just be easier to keep the original paper than to waste time rewriting everything in the planning notebook? Excuses, excuses—and I thought we took care of that problem chapters ago!

Think about it. Putting the paper away, shuffling around it in the meantime, and finding it again (hopefully before the deadline) will take a lot longer and cause a lot more mental stress than writing it once and forgetting about it until it comes up on your calendar. Just try it and prove it to yourself.

You have to attend a staff meeting next Tuesday. Whenever you think of a subject for discussion or a question you want answered, you reach for separate pieces of scratch paper and keep them on your desk spindle until meeting time. Right? Wrong. Open your calendar to next Tuesday, the day of the meeting, and begin a list of items you want to bring up. Every time you think of something else, add it to the list. When the day of the meeting arrives, you'll be efficiently prepared. No searching for notes or reminders and no forgetting an important point.

This same idea works for trips or vacations. Start a to-take list on the date you'll be packing for the trip. Whenever you think of something you must take with you, add it to the list. When packing day rolls around, *voila!* There's your list of things to bring, ready and waiting for action.

Your oldest son is a busboy at the Miyako Restaurant. Your younger son asks, "Mom, what's a busboy?" After explaining the job description, your little boy says with a laugh, "I thought a busboy was a guy who met people as they got off the bus and tried to get them to eat at the Miyako."

Where do you record all the cute things the kids say, when they take their first steps, and when they say their first words? Where do you write the details and feelings you experience after an especially trying day, or the joys you share after a hard-fought victory? Yes, you guessed it. You record these things in the calendar section of your planning notebook. It's the perfect place to make diary or journal entries.

Here are some more examples: You're cleaning out the basement, and you find Marilyn's folding chairs that you borrowed on New Year's Eve. You toss the chairs into the car and return them to Marilyn.

A few hours later you notice the nozzle has blown off the end of the hose. You put the hose in the car and head to the garden center for the needed repair.

Later, stumbling over Jim's Big Wheel (Jim, by the way, is fourteen now), you think maybe little Benjie down the street would like to have it. So you toddle down the road and win Benjie's undying love and devotion.

Well, so far, if I were keeping score, I'd say you're batting 1,000. In other words: wrong, wrong, wrong. Here's why: You should clean with your calendar!

Put Marilyn's chairs in the corner and make a note in your running to-do list to return them to her. Wait. Hold it right there. All of a sudden you remember that you're going over to Marilyn's Thursday afternoon to see her new dining-room set. Instead of lengthening the running to-do list, just turn to Thursday's page in your calendar and write "Return Marilyn's folding chairs." That way you're beginning to build

Thursday's daily action plan in advance. And when Thursday rolls around, you're automatically reminded to return the chairs.

As for the hose, put it where it belongs and add a note on the running to-do list that it needs to be repaired. Then put the Big Wheel beside the folding chairs and write in your calendar another reminder (or ask one of your kids to take the bike to Benjie and be done with it).

With this method, it's easy to see how you have shaved hours from basement cleaning time. Clean with your calendar. (Or, use your head to save your heels!)

On my monthly calendars I record dates, deadlines, appointments, birthdays, anniversaries, the last time I watered the plants, 6 month dental check-ups, etc. It's just a fast glance or index to my month. More detailed information about any one of these events is listed on the daily calendar pages. On this page is a section for today's to do list, appointments and notes. In the notes section of the page I record things like journal or diary entries, recipes, vacation to-take lists, meeting notes, baseball sign-up information, mileage, business expenses, etc.

Here's my daily routine.

For the most part, I plan my days the night before. However, when to plan is a personal decision. I prefer evenings over mornings because I've found that in the morning I plan under pressure. I need to get the kids up, dressed, fed, and out the door. Ditto for me! The phone rings, the baby cries, the beds are unmade. My inclination at that point is to get busy. Planning can wait. However, in the evening I'm more objective and can see what jobs are truly important. Instead of just getting busy with whatever, I plan according to long-term considerations.

I take a few minutes at the end of the day to review what I have done and to evaluate my performance. If my plans have gone awry, I ask myself why. Then I compare the way I have actually used my time with the way I intended to use it. If the day has been a disaster, I think of things I could have done to make the outcome different. I make notes in my calendar of the things that have come along that have thrown a wrench in my plans. Usually, I discover that it's my own lack of prioritizing and sticking to my priorities that gets me in trouble.

Next, I decide what I must get done tomorrow. I look at any dates, deadlines, and appointments I have scheduled and determine how much time I have to work with. If I'm going to be in a meeting all day, my daily action plan will be fairly short. On days when I have several hours to work with, my list is considerably longer.

Then I check my goals section and ask, "What can I do today to bring that goal out of the future and a little closer to realization?" Since I'm working a physical fitness goal, "aerobic video" is part of my daily action plan. Improving my level of spirituality is also a goal, so "pray and read scriptures" are two more items noted on the to-do list.

Always keeping my time schedule in mind, I choose as many goal activities as possible. Then I check the running to-do list and select a few of those jobs. Since I'm going to the mall this afternoon, I can pick up the wedding present for Steve and Sally. I'll call Judy and see if she wants to meet me for lunch at the Thai Foon Restaurant. Since I'll be driving past the garden center, I'll also get the hose fixed. All of a sudden, three things have been checked off the running to-do list.

Now, referring to my housekeeping schedule, I list any household jobs that need to be taken care of. If I'm delegating any of those chores, I also note the initials of the assigned person. That way I can more effectively follow through to see if the job has been done. It's also a relief to see something on the list that *I* don't have to worry about.

So, there's your list in a neat linear line written on your calendar. You plan to start at the top and work your way down. But first do you do something easy just to get it out of the way, and then make a few phone calls? No! No! No!

First, take a look at your list. Some of the tasks will be maintenance activities that just keep you caught up (such as housework, fixing the hose) while others will be achievement activities (prayer, reading scriptures, aerobic exercise). If your list is filled with maintenance activities only, take some of them off and replace them with at least one achievement task. Filling their days with nothing but maintenance chores is probably the main reason many women do not feel fulfilled at home. It's the maintaining we do day in and day out that discourages us and makes us feel overwhelmed.

Maintenance is vital, though. It keeps things running smoothly and adds to a pleasant feeling of contentment at home. But over-maintenance is deadly. If you overdo it, people will go somewhere else when they want to enjoy themselves. There are institutions everywhere that will accept your family members exactly as they are—dirty shoes and all. Our homes need to be welcoming and inviting too.

Now, where do you draw the line? Here's what I do. One year we were having an office Christmas party at our house. *Everything will be perfect*, I dreamed. I planned a two-week cleaning spree to organize every closet, every cupboard, every drawer. There would not be found so much as a cobweb hanging from a single stud in the basement. The storage boxes would be neatly stacked and organized, the filing caught up, the snow blower polished. And so I planned.

Then reality (and the Christmas season) hit with full force. Brian made the basketball team. Drive to practices, attend games. Jim, Jr., who doesn't drive, got a job twenty minutes away from home. More driving. Christmas shopping. Holiday baking. Steven's band concert. My job. Rehearse for the Christmas program at church. Make gifts for the children in my Sunday School class. And to top it off, I needed to clean the basement, file, scrub, organize, and entertain. I was getting tense and anxious and was snapping at Jim and the kids. I couldn't have been under more pressure had I been asked to repaint the Sistine chapel. What was I doing to myself?

"OK," I said to myself, "what's my goal?" Since the party preparations were causing me the most stress and pressure, I started with that one.

"I want everyone to have a good time and to feel welcomed," I replied. "I want to be an efficient but warm hostess. I want the house to be neat enough so as not to embarrass us." What did filing have to do with my goal? What about the storage boxes? The cobwebs in the basement? The kids' closets? NOTHING.

So, I altered my original plan to suit my goal. The pressure was lifted. We had the party and it was a rousing success—even though the basement looked like a garage sale in progress.

Here's my point: Perfection is only necessary when it directly relates to a goal. Suppose I was taking a group of people through my home to demonstrate how a home should be cleaned and organized. In that case, my original party-cleaning plan would be necessary. Sure, I still need to clean my basement and catch up on the filing, but now I've scheduled those chores for the week after I've finished this manuscript. Whenever I run out of day before I run out of list, I ask, "What's my goal?" and I go for the most important and directly related tasks.

Let's look at the item on my list that reads "Make gifts for the children in my Sunday School class." Now, there are ten children in that class, and making gifts for each child would take a lot of time. What was my goal? I wanted to give each of the children a present for Christmas. In order to achieve that goal, did the gifts have to be handmade? No. Thus, I set my goal: buy the gifts.

Now, if my goal had been "Make Christmas gifts for my Sunday School class so their parents will be impressed with my handiwork and realize how much time I spend on those kids," then handmade gifts would have been important. Or, if the goal had mentioned saving money, handmade gifts would likely have been one way to meet that requirement.

Imagine two pint jars sitting side by side. The jar on the left contains three golf balls, representing your goal or achievement activities. The jar on the right is three-fourths full of popcorn kernels, representing all the maintenance activities you do repeatedly every day. If you take the golf balls out of their jar and try to put them into the jar with the popcorn, they won't fit, will they? But try it the other way and see what happens. Put the golf balls back into their jar and pour the kernels over them. Somehow, as if by magic, the kernels and the balls fit in the same container.

In other words, if the achievement activities are done first, there will still be room for the maintenance activities—at least for the most important ones.

I don't want to belabor the point. Just remember, when you're stressed out, to step back, look at your list, and ask, "What's my goal?" Then eliminate the excess baggage. Any jobs that don't directly contribute to the desired and ultimate outcome should be cast aside—at least for now.

To keep yourself on track, number the entries on your daily action plan in the order they should be done and check them off as they're completed. Items left unfinished can be assigned to another day or returned to the running to-do section, if you're not sure when you'll be able to get to them.

Nailing things down in writing is requisite to a functional time-management system. Plan ahead. Assign priorities. Keep track of your dates, deadlines, and appointments. Make a daily action plan. Review your time use.

Your best moments are when you feel in control. Follow this simple time-management program and enjoy days on end of feeling on top of things. You will discover greater freedom and relaxation and develop a large measure of control over your time and your destiny. As free time begins to unfold, you'll notice that it is unclouded by the uneasy awareness of tasks undone and anxiety about the future. It's just common sense that planning can't help but bring you more of what you want in life.

6

Many Hands Make Light Work

Learn to Delegate

Delegation. The word evokes myriad images—tears, tantrums, and threats. Turbulence, tattling, and tension. Nothing, save the word *no*, elicits such a response from children. And it's that dreaded reaction that keeps fainthearted folks (like me) from delegating chores in the first place. But delegate we must.

Directing the heavy traffic created by housework and homework, kids and careers, meals and meetings—all the while trying to have a Fonda-fit body—it's no wonder things often get lost in the scramble, such as your time, your mental health, and perhaps a navy blue sandal or two. Yes, today's lifestyles make delegating obligatory. Why, even a big wheel needs spokes.

Now I was going to wait awhile before making this astounding declaration, but I can hold back no longer. It's excruciating. It's like knowing Mary Poppins is looking for work, having her phone number, and never calling it. Take a look at today's action plan and ask yourself, "Do each of these jobs need to be done by me or do they just need to be completed?" That, in a nutshell, is the very cornerstone of delegation: realizing that you don't have to do it all.

Many people think that effective time management means doing everything faster so *you* can squeeze it all in. Not so. I know, I know. If we could only convince the family. I'm going to let you in on a little secret. Most likely everyone in your home thinks the housework is *your* work, *your* responsibility. And how do I know that? Because I used to be a kid once too.

I was reared in a family of six children, and as a result, there was always a lot that needed to be done around the house. Every Saturday morning I was the last kid on the block to get outside to play, because my housework had to come first. Every Saturday morning I would mumble as I dusted, mumble as I straightened my chest of drawers, and mumble as I dried dishes. "If she (meaning Mother) didn't want to do this stuff, why did she get married in the first place?"

Now, as an adult, I am ashamed of those feelings, yet very grateful for a mother who let me mumble and grumble to my heart's content, for I learned two important lessons: I work before play, and I let my own children complain, gripe, and whine. (Like Mother always said: "You get back what you dish out.")

I know you're an intelligent person. You don't need a lecture and an itemized list giving you the rules of effective delegation. What you do need, though, are a few ideas to help you break down the wall of resistance that stands between you, the delegator, and your child, the delegatee.

The most important ingredient is to foster an atmosphere of cooperation. Stay off the child's back. Don't harp. Don't nag. Don't play the martyr. Be positive in your approach.

"Mom, will you help me with my campaign posters?"

"Sure, I'd love to. But I need to finish these few things on my list first. If you want to help I'll be done sooner."

Or, "Mom, Matt and I want to go bowling. Can you drive us down and pick us up too?"

"Steven, you've been so helpful this week and given me so much free time, I'll be glad to give you and Matt a ride."

We have to let our children know that we have the time to help them because they've helped us. They don't automatically understand that. We need to let them know that there's a direct correlation between our availability and their cooperation.

Whenever possible, get the children mentally prepared for what lies ahead. That is a stellar reason for using the planning sheets recommended in chapter 5. The children pre-agree to everything listed on those sheets and know a week in advance what is expected of them during the week.

How much cooperation do you breed in a situation like this: Susan walks in the front door after school and announces, "A bunch of us are going to McDonald's. We'll be back in an hour or so."

"Not so fast, young lady. You're not leaving this house until I can see the floor in your bedroom. And that includes the floor under your bed and in the closet!"

Had Susan known a week in advance that she had to clean her room she could have made different plans with her friends, or she could have cleaned the room sooner than you required.

Planning sheets eliminate a lot of unnecessary prodding. When your children ask if they can go outside and play, say simply, "Go check your planning sheet and see if everything is done."

For children who can't read, draw simple pictures, cut out photos from magazines, or assign an older child to read their assignments to them.

Another way to nurture this cooperative spirit is to explain your methods for doing things. When family members can see and understand your logic rather than assume it's idiosyncrasy, they are more likely to cooperate.

Here's an example. We store little storybooks in a large plastic dishpan. The books are standing up with the covers facing forward, which permits the child to flip through the collection and pull out the book of his choice without having to dump the trove all over the floor. The system has worked flawlessly for years until our daughter, Schuyler, started toddling around. By the time she was two and a half, she was still pouring out the whole pan of books whenever she wanted to hear a story.

I knew this was an effective storage method. For years it had served me faithfully and weathered the abuse of four boys who, collectively, had been a whirling dervish of activity. Why, oh why, was it not working for our quiet little girl?

Finally it occurred to me that she had never been taught the system. So, I spent about two minutes showing her how to browse through the entire collection without having to dump it. End of problem.

What may seem obvious to you may not be quite as clear to one of your children. Explain how things are done and why they're done in a particular fashion.

Too bad children aren't born with a guarantee that says, "This child will self-maintain in five years. He will make his bed, pick up his clothes, put his toys away, and always put a matching pair of socks in the clothes hamper." Imagine the reduction in your work load if every person were to self-maintain. Ahhhhhhh.

Perhaps this beatific state will never quite materialize, but you can certainly nourish the dream by incorporating systems that are easy for the child to implement. Here are some ideas:

1. Shoes will be put away if they can be thrown into a large open container. I've never seen a kid yet who'll file his

shoes into a shoe file, tuck them into a shoe bag, or slide them onto shoe racks. But give him a large container (cardboard box, kitty-litter pan, or industrial-sized dishpan) and it works every time. Of course, in the dishpan the shoes aren't necessarily standing at attention in neatly matched pairs. But they are contained and confined, easy to put away and instantly located.

2. Have in/out baskets for each child. When the children come home from school, they toss their books and papers into their bins. When they receive magazines, mail, or packages from Grandma, toss them into their in/out baskets. When you sign permission slips, report cards, or "please excuse" notes, put them into the respective containers. Homework is never lost and hunted for, the kitchen counter is kept clutter free, and self-maintenance is a snap. (More on school papers in chapter 14.) Where to put these bins? If you haven't a spare shelf in the kitchen, the lowest shelf in the linen closet works perfectly. These bins are so vital, any space you make to accommodate them is well worth it.

3. Every child needs a junk drawer or some kind of container without a lid—a kitty-litter pan, a restaurant-sized dishpan, a cardboard box. Here's where the child tosses the license plate from the box of Honeycombs. The cardboard backing from the newest G.I. Joe. A gumball ring. A Pez dispenser. A 1984 Texas Folklife Festival pin. All are candidates for the junk container. (If space is at a premium, keep the box under the child's bed. And, most important, when containers are full, something must be tossed out in order to make room for new items.)

4. Children not only have junk "things"—they also have junk paper. To a son, of course, the 1982 Chicago Bulls basketball schedule is *not* junk. Nor is that letter he wrote to James Bond or the note he got from his girlfriend. These valuable documents need a place, and the perfect container is a magazine file. This kind of file is usually made from heavy cardboard and is available at most large discount stores

and office-supply outlets. Or you can recycle a cereal or laundry detergent box and make your own.

5. Take the sting out of the words "Clean up that room!" by introducing the child to a quick clean-up technique. Here's how it works:

The next time one of your kids has to clean his room, give him a trash bag and a laundry basket. Tell him that the fastest way to finish the job is to stay in the room until it's clean, and the trash bag and laundry basket are to help him. All trash—old school papers, dried-out food, wrappers, and so forth—goes into the trash bag. Dirty laundry is put into the laundry basket. Next, anything that belongs in another room (dirty dishes, sister's doll, snowsuit, piano music, video tapes, and so forth) are placed just outside the bedroom door in the hall. When everything is tidy, he dumps the trash, deposits the laundry, and puts away all the cast-offs waiting in the hallway. (Once the laundry basket is emptied, he can use it as a tote box to help him deliver all those "put aways.")

For young children, I've found it's a lot less frustrating to put the toys away once a day rather than to follow the kids around the house and continually tidy up after them. When toys are left lying in the family room, living room, or other common-area room, toss them into a large basket, plastic wastebasket, or large drawstring bag. (For safety reasons, large plastic trash bags are not recommended.) Then, just before bed, have the children help you return each toy to its rightful location.

Here are a few more ideas that simplify frequently delegated chores:

- Basic accessories such as a trash basket and clothes hamper in each bedroom encourage self-maintenance.
- Low-hanging closet rods and low shelves scale down a child's room and make related tasks more manageable.

- Use drawer dividers to separate socks, T-shirts, pajamas, and underwear.
- For small children, paste pictures on drawer dividers so they know what article goes where.

To avoid morning madness, set out tomorrow's clothes the night before. Hang matching outfits and accessories (kept in a small drawstring bag) on the same hanger. School-aged children should each have an alarm clock and be responsible for getting themselves out of bed. (Some children who are difficult to rouse may require two or three alarm clocks set at 5-minute intervals.) That way you won't end up wasting a lot of your morning cajoling a child out of bed.

I suppose the most commonly delegated chore is dishes. Here again, make it easy. Jobs like setting and clearing the table or loading and unloading the dishwasher are simplified when dishes, flatware, and glasses are toted back and forth in a dishpan.

Once the simplified systems are executed, work with the kids. As they become older and more competent, you can begin to withdraw from some of your responsibilities. For example, I work with the children in the kitchen just long enough for them to know what to do and where to put things. For the first little while they'll say, "Where does this casserole dish go? What about the cake pan and the colander? How do you load the dishwasher?"

Remember, even working with the kids is faster than doing the entire job yourself and further nourishes the cooperative attitude. In a nutshell, here's a rundown:

- Encourage a feeling of cooperation.
- Get the children mentally prepared.
- Explain why things are done a certain way.
- Set up simple organizational systems.
- Work with the children and teach them what to do.

Nevertheless, beware. Children are masters at upward delegation—trying to get you to take the job back. Pay attention to the creative ways your children do it; by ignoring their attempts, you'll stop the game.

Our nine-year-old gripes. Boy, does he gripe. With the drama of a soap-opera heroine he feigns illness. As if auditioning for a remake of *Roots*, he moans, "Why do I have to do all the work around here?" Bondage and slavery are his bywords. If this kid doesn't make it as a professional complainer, the Grand Canyon will never make it as a professional hole!

Schuyler's method is somewhat subtle. Curling her lower lip and blinking back tears, she laments, "I hate housework."

Our oldest teenager, who at this writing is seventeen years old, asks questions—and lots of them! In the years since his birth, I've fielded more questions than Ann Landers. Get this: A week ago he said—and I promise this is true—"Mom, how do you make a bed?"

He figures that if he asks enough questions and interrupts me often enough, I'll decide it's easier to do it myself or come to his rescue and be relieved of the cross-examination. I'll admit it, his method worked for quite a while until I got wise to his tactics. Now, I just say, "I'm sure you'll figure it out."

Stop feeling sorry for the "poor little things." Generally speaking, any behavior resembling that of a Libyan leader, a three-year-old child, and a professional tennis star is usually just a cleverly disguised attempt at upward delegation. Express your heartfelt confidence in the child's ability and leave him to his work.

Once in a while plaintive cries are signals that the child has not been trained properly. Had Jim, Jr., been six years old and not made his bed several times before, his bed-making question would have been acceptable.

So, determine the cause of the kids' protests. If they've been trained and you've seen them succeed at the job, you may well assume the problem is upward delegation. If not, perhaps more training is required. Kids and organization are not, contrary to popular belief, mutually exclusive. But to happily marry the two does take some work on your part. No matter what else you do, appreciate their efforts.

My husband does a lot of dishes and almost always puts them away in the wrong places. So what? It takes me one or two minutes to straighten things out. But without his help I'd be spending thirty or forty-five minutes in the kitchen. Be grateful for anything anyone does to help, because every minute the other person invests is a minute you save.

Perhaps relying on family members alone is not the whole answer. No, I'm not going to suggest that you go without sleep in order to squeeze a few extra hours into your day. You're probably sacrificing sleep already. And, no, you don't have to accept a lower standard of household upkeep. Another solution is to delegate the most annoying and time-consuming chores by hiring outside help.

Here's a list of duties to consider hiring out: housework, yard work, laundry and ironing, mending and sewing, grocery shopping, cooking, pet care, chauffeuring and errand running, window washing, car maintenance, plant care, house repairs, bookkeeping.

Who's available for these types of jobs? Students, homemakers, retired people, and, of course, professional housekeepers and cleaning services.

Students, homemakers, and retirees usually have more flexible schedules, are willing to work short-hour jobs, and generally charge less per hour than the professionals. The professionals, however, are usually bonded and insured.

To locate a qualified candidate check the following sources:

1. *Schools.* Call the guidance counselors at your local junior and senior high schools. They may have a listing of students who are seeking work. The counselor is also aware of the students' work habits, personality traits, and dependability, all of which are of interest to you as an employer.

2. *Senior citizen centers.* If there is a center in your area, call to see if they offer referral services for retirees. Other

places to check are libraries and community centers.

3. *Friends*. Talk to your friends and co-workers. Do they know someone who does the kind of work you're requiring? One of my friends is a housekeeper who has never had to advertise. She started working for one woman and before long had more business than she alone could handle. Word of mouth is a good source of reliable help.

4. *Community*. Local newspapers are an obvious source of help either by searching the situations-wanted section in the want ads or placing an ad yourself. Other community sources are bulletin boards found in some supermarkets, laundromats, photocopy outlets, and student union buildings on college campuses. The yellow pages of the phone book will also give a quick rundown on professionals in your area.

Interview all potential candidates and make special note of each one's appearance, personality, and suitability for the particular job. Be sure to check references from previous employers, and always talk to at least one character reference (neighbor, religious leader, a close friend, or out-of-state family member).

When you've singled out the right helper, strike an agreement. Determine how often and how long he or she will work in a week. Whenever possible, set specific starting and stopping hours. Salary and salary reviews should also be discussed and agreed upon. Consider, too, how sick days will be handled. Above all, though, be sure there is a clear-cut job description so both parties will know what to expect.

Now you have the principles of delegating firmly within your grasp. Persist and be patient, for the rewards are many. Delegating is like a stone thrown into a pool. Just as the ripples spread out in ever-widening circles, so the benefits of delegation can expand and enrich your life.

You'll make time for yourself and your family, which in turn will create a harmonious lifestyle and bring the balance back into your life. Delegate and make time for the good times. It's time well spent.

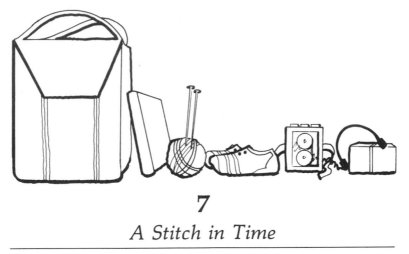

7

A Stitch in Time

Make Every Moment Count

Once upon a time there was a mayonnaise manufacturer with a problem. He was producing large quantities of mayonnaise, which use a lot of egg yolks; but the more mayonnaise he produced, the more egg whites he had left over. Day after day he watched helplessly as his workers discarded hundreds of pounds of egg whites.

Finally he turned the problem over to one of his chemists and asked him if he could figure out a resourceful way to use all those egg whites. After some time the chemist returned with a fine by-product that did indeed use a lot of egg whites. He invented marshmallows—and now you know the rest of the story.

This wise manufacturer wasn't satisfied with leaving well enough alone. He wanted to use up the odds and ends, the leftovers. He wanted to squeeze a measure of value out of everything he possibly could. Often the success of an industry depends upon its ability to develop and use by-products. Even movies and TV shows have spin-offs that result in new programs. Meat packers use every portion of an animal for some useful purpose—the hooves for glue and the hair for strong rope, and so forth. And where would we be without the by-products of the oil industry? Imagine not having gasoline or plastic.

The little minutes of our lives, the odd moments, are the by-products of our time. And our success also depends upon our ability to use them. Those who are most successful in life are usually those who wisely use odd moments.

I became a moment manager very modestly at first by always carrying some handwork with me whenever I left the house. Before long I had crocheted doilies to put under baskets, plants, and figurines. Almost miraculously badges were sewn (rather than stapled) onto Scout uniforms. I even managed to cross-stitch a special message to a friend.

But the real payoff was Schuyler's Christmas dress. I finished it *before* Christmas! It was a long crocheted dress covered with ruffles. The skirt alone was fifty-five inches around and thirty-six inches long. Six weeks before Christmas I decided it would be impossible to finish that dress, but with my newfound resolve to use up every odd moment, and with the determination of a trash compactor, I did it.

Of course, I was terribly proud of myself and began to brag just a little by telling everyone how much could be accomplished in a minute here and there. I soon discovered, as braggarts do, that I was only an amateur. There are a lot of pros who do very little talking about their efforts. Instead, they parlay every extra second into something productive and worthwhile.

For example, the president of a major university reads while waiting for a stoplight to turn green. A mother of eleven children teaches her daughters to knit at the age of three. An expert quilter whips up a masterpiece while she's waiting for something to happen. One woman keeps a copy of the Bible in her laundry room and during the course of a few years she reads the entire book while she's waiting for the spin cycle to finish.

I met another pro at a meeting I had spoken at. She approached me cautiously, not realizing that she was addressing an amateur, for it was she who taught me. "For years," she confessed, "magazines piled up around the house unread. I just couldn't find enough time to sit down and read them." So this clever minute manager put the magazines in the bathroom and read them cover to cover every single month by reading one article, one poem, one story at a time. Another miracle of the odd moment.

Then there's my friend Sherrill Anderson. She's a working wife and mother who still makes time for personal development. During lunch hours and coffee breaks, you'll often find Sherrill tackling some kind of project—perhaps errands, paperwork, shopping, or handicrafts. When she's talking on the phone or waiting in the dentist's office, you can bet she's doing something. One particularly complicated and beautiful cross-stitch sampler graces her home. She worked on it during pack meetings. And with three boys, she goes to plenty of those.

Sherrill's home is filled with her handiwork. So are the homes of her friends. Handmade Christmas gifts and birthday remembrances, messages of encouragement, and cheering phone calls are all a part of her life, made possible by the odd moment.

In five short months, again using up the odd moments, she painted all the doors, woodwork, crown moldings, and baseboards in her home (which required removing and relaying carpet, a job she also did by herself); repapered her bathroom, bedroom, entry way, and stairway; upholstered the headboard of her bed and made matching throw pillows; converted a front hall closet into a pantry; cleaned out her basement; and organized a neighborhood garage sale—in addition to several other projects I am too tired to mention. One

"Good morning!" from Sherrill and I have the sudden urge to dust the water softener, tailor a suit, and finish the Christmas shopping by the Fourth of July! Everyone should have such an invigorating friendship.

Yes, *these* are the pros, the real achievers, and *my* passing along time-management advice was like pointing out middle C to the Mormon Tabernacle Choir. I was an Oscar Madison in a world filled with Felix Ungers. But at least I was on the right track.

As I studied and watched these master minute managers I noticed a common denominator. They anticipate events. Anticipatory planning not only gives them extra chunks of free time, it also helps them absorb every odd moment with productive activity. Now, I am not suggesting that every minute of your day be saturated with productive activity. I use odd moments for *fun*. I crochet, pore over cookbooks, knit, read, eat, and so on. And sometimes I use odd moments to chip away at a large task so I'll have a block of free time later on.

The first thing I learned to anticipate was waiting time. Have you ever noticed how much of your day is spent waiting for something to happen? You wait for the water to boil, wait for an appointment, wait for the bus, wait in line at the grocery store, wait for the kids at school, practices, and lessons. Each one of us spends a lot of time waiting every single day.

And it often happens unexpectedly. I was scheduled to attend a meeting that was being held at a local library. The meeting started at 9:00 A.M., so I arrived at 8:40 A.M. to register and get settled in. Imagine my surprise when the librarians refused to unlock the doors before nine o'clock. Why didn't I bring something to do?

It was my turn to carpool the basketball team after practice. I pulled up behind the gym at 5:00 P.M., the time the boys were always finished. But for some reason they didn't leave practice until 5:30 that evening. Why didn't I bring something to do?

I made a doctor's appointment and intentionally scheduled the first appointment time of the day so I wouldn't have
to wait. Guess what—I know, I should have known better—
someone had a baby and you know who had to deliver it.
Why didn't I bring something to do?

Yes, I've learned through experience to always carry something with me that will occupy my time should I find myself
waiting. And I bring it even when I'm positive I won't have
to wait.

First, I always have my planning notebook with me. That
gives me a book to both read and write in. Inside my book
are thought-provoking messages to read and enjoy. A list of
words and their meanings are ready for review. With my
planning notebook I can plan tomorrow, re-read a goal, work
out menus and prepare a shopping list, or record a journal
entry. There's lots to do when you have a planning notebook
with you.

Next, I always carry my waiting bag when I'm commut-
ing on public transportation or going somewhere in the car.
What's a waiting bag? It holds anything you want it to, but
here's what I keep in mine.

My waiting bag is a red gym bag that holds a craft project
I'm working on. Everything from an afghan to a penguin has
been toted around in that carry-all. I keep all the needed
supplies for the project, including directions, right in the
satchel. A small cosmetic bag holds crochet hooks, scissors,
tape measure, stitch holders and markers, and a variety of
needles.

I use the waiting bag at home too. I carry it into the
family room so I can sit down and work on my project while
I watch TV. Everything is self-contained, and I never have to
run around searching for materials.

What if you're not crafty? The waiting bag can hold mending, books, office work, reading that has to be done for your
job (trade journals, professional articles, newsletters), newspapers and magazines, letter-writing supplies, cassette recorder
and tapes (these can also be used for dictation), paperwork,

a warm-up suit, and running shoes. Virtually any portable task is a nominee for the waiting bag.

Another defense weapon is my car organizer. I use a plastic pencil box type container because it's compact yet roomy, shuts tightly, and slips easily under the front seat of the car. Inside the organizer I keep a few pieces of stationery, some envelopes, stamps, Band-Aids, wet wiping cloths, purse-size package of facial tissue, scissors, pens, a mending kit, loose change, glue, tape, stapler and staples, a paper punch, paper clips, and a memo pad. A few minutes spent putting this kit together has saved me hours of time and prevented many needless frustrations. Being prepared is the answer to most of life's crises!

Another thing I carry is my "handbag office." This is a very small, zippered cosmetic bag I keep in my handbag. It holds a small roll of tape, a miniature paper punch (so I can punch floating pieces of paper and include them in my planning notebook), tiny (and I mean tiny) stapler and staples, small scissors, rubber bands, tape measure, Post-It notes, and paper clips. This purse office is approximately 4 x 5 inches (just slightly larger than an index card) and is about three-fourths of an inch thick. It's very small but extremely useful.

Now I find myself planning waiting time. I try to be early for meetings and appointments. That way I have a few minutes of uninterrupted time to work on the project in my waiting bag. I've found, though, that (weather permitting) the best place to wait is in the car. It's quiet and you won't be interrupted. There's no one to talk to and nothing to keep you from your chosen task. (Of course, if it's a doctor's appointment you don't want to wait in the car. Get in that office as soon as possible and put your name on the waiting list—now!)

The media tours I did for Procter and Gamble gave me many opportunities to wait. Flying from city to city and waiting to board planes gave me countless hours of uninterrupted time. Waiting in TV studios for a scheduled appearance and filling lonely hours in a hotel room, I chalked up still more time.

One particular trip I decided I'd knit a winter coat for Schuyler, so I packed up my waiting bag and carried it with me on the plane. At the city of my destination I met my publicist, who gave me a quick rundown of our week's activities and then whisked me off to our hotel. Determined to have the coat finished by the end of the week, I was knitting as we drove.

"I used to love to knit," Sally sighed. "I had a sweater started, but I gave it up. I just don't have time to knit anymore."

For four full days Sally and I were together. I knit at TV and radio stations, in airports, in hotel rooms, and 35,000 feet in the air as we flew from one city to another. Sally read, slept, ate, and talked—yet she didn't have time to knit. Of course she had time. She had just chosen other activities.

However, if you sincerely wish you had time for a once-beloved hobby, start anticipating waiting time and use it. It's amazing how much you can accomplish even when you have to chip away at something. (Yes, I finished the coat.)

Once you've mastered waiting time, look for other ways anticipatory planning can help you whittle away unnecessary demands on your time budget and your nerves.

My family is not too great at planning ahead, so I check with everyone the night before and ask them what their plans are for tomorrow. I'm mainly interested in any event that directly concerns me and affects my time.

For example, Jim might say, "I'm playing racketball at 5:30 tomorrow evening." Red alert. Knowing Jim as I do, at 5:15 he's going to ask me if his trunks are clean. And, "Do you know where I put my racket? Where's my gym bag? Did Brian use my glove when he was playing baseball?" So, I get everything situated now instead of waiting for the inevitable upheaval at 5:15 tomorrow evening.

"Oh, yeah, Mom. I was late for school yesterday and you need to write a note." I do it *now* instead of waiting for tomorrow's rush hour.

"I'm staying after school to watch a volleyball game. Can you come and get me?" I schedule it *now*, or make other arrangements for the child to get home.

This is a good time to review what dates, deadlines, and appointments you have scheduled for tomorrow. Now is the time to scan the kids' planning sheets to see if you've overlooked something.

Do you see how anticipatory planning eliminates a lot of unnecessary interruptions and last-minute hassles? It allows you to spend some time now so you won't have to be interrupted later on. You can schedule your day's activities around these other responsibilities.

What else can you anticipate? Will your children be invited to birthday parties in upcoming months? Do you always buy gifts for specific friends or loved ones? Do you send greeting cards? If you know that you're going to need things such as gifts and cards, why do you waste time making special trips to the store whenever a special event comes up? Anticipate these events. Shop sales and stockpile gifts and cards to have on hand.

Frequently people use money as an excuse for procrastinating. If you don't have the money now, the only reason you'll have it later is because it's urgent. ("Mom's birthday is tomorrow. I *have* to buy her gift today.") Also, if you find good sales, sometimes several gifts add up to less money than one gift would cost at the regular price.

A few weeks ago I was browsing through a store and saw several travel kits that were being discontinued. I knew they'd make wonderful gifts so I checked the price. They were marked down, incredibly, to $1.00, so I bought five of them and stored them in a gift box at home. Another time I found an irresistible music box marked down from $14.00 to $1.98. (Yes, it worked and was in mint condition.) I found some full-color, large picture books for children, regularly

$6.95, that were marked down to $1.50. I bought four for birthday gifts and spent less than had I bought one at the regular price.

You see, "I don't have enough money," is not always a valid excuse. Once you have a gift supply at home to draw from, save a little money now and then so you'll have a small cash reserve when these wonderful sales come along.

Saving money, I suppose, is reason enough to anticipate buying gifts, but just wait until you see how much time you'll save. No more unnecessary trips to the store. You'll always be prepared. Time management is truly the most effective weapon in your battle against stress.

What else can you anticipate? Think of anything that comes up on a regular basis—car inspections, spelling tests every Friday, bills to pay, Christmas, income taxes, planting the garden, Sunday dinner. All can be planned for and executed flawlessly without tension or trauma.

Have you ever noticed how we gasp in horror when we read that someone has thrown away his whole life through a single act of suicide? Yet we each throw our lives away a minute here, a minute there, and we think nothing of it.

Please commit the following statements to memory, then raise your right hand and promise to remember them always:

1. Self-discipline comes through anticipatory planning, not when the time of decision arrives.

2. No one has enough time to use only ideal moments.

3. Don't let an imperfect situation be an excuse to do nothing.

Anticipate and liberate!

8

Putting Off Procrastination

Do It Right—Right Now

For today's test, please complete the following sentence: As salt is to pepper, as ham is to egg, as bread is to butter, procrastination is to: (a) chewed fingernails, (b) conniption fits, (c) medical calamities, such as high blood pressure, stroke, upset stomach, nervous prostration, headache, or depression, (d) botchery, (e) all of the above, but especially medical calamities and botchery.

If you didn't pick E, you are hereby banned for life from watching anything on TV except fly fishing. Shame on you. Don't you know how harmful procrastination is to your well-being? Rumor has it that the surgeon general has taken the procrastination problem under advisement and is expected to issue a warning soon.

I confess. Many years ago, I would have chosen (a) chewed fingernails too. In those days I was only mildly aware of the price I was paying for my procrastination. But I've gotten myself into so many jams because of putting things off that I've come to realize that procrastination is a deadly time, energy, and money (yes, money) destroyer.

I suffer from a disease similar to alcoholism in that there is no cure except admitting your addiction and abstinence. I am, gulp, an "as soon as-er." As soon as Schuyler gets into high school, I'll clean the basement and catch up the baby books. As soon as I do the dishes, make the beds, vacuum, and clean the bathroom, I'll start my daily planning session. As soon as I take a nap, I'll get up and exercise. As soon as I can afford it, I'll take piano lessons again. I've wasted a lot of todays waiting for the perfect tomorrow. And so it goes.

Along with todays, a lot of cold, hard cash is also wasted. In Utah we are required to have our cars undergo a yearly safety inspection. Well, one year we "didn't have time" to do it before the deadline, so we decided to press our luck for a day or two. Just as we began to press, we were, of course, stopped by a friendly police officer. Listening to the lecture and waiting while he wrote the ticket took about twenty minutes. Then we had approximately ten days to drive out to city hall and pay the fine. (Add another hour and subtract thirty dollars.) And you know what? We still had to get the car inspected. Did we save any time procrastinating? No. The very act of putting off the job added an additional one hour and twenty minutes and cost us an extra thirty dollars. The thirty dollars, by the way, reflects only the cost of the fine and not the loss in wages that occurred when we took off work to take care of that little matter.

A woman attending one of my classes related this costly account: "My husband rented a hydraulic jack and kept putting off returning it to the rental agency. Day after day the rental payments accrued until the agency finally called and said they needed to receive a payment and the jack—unless my husband wanted to continue renting it. He returned the jack and tried to beg off the rental fee by saying he hadn't been using the jack and that he had simply forgotten to return it. The upshot of the story is that ultimately the man was sued by the rental agency and not only had to pay the bill but also hire an attorney and miss work to go to court. The total cost of his procrastination? Approximately thirty-five hundred dollars and fifteen hours of his time.

Let's face it. None of us has the time or the money to procrastinate. For the most part, I've kicked the habit, and perhaps this would be a nice time to share with you the ten best antiprocrastination measures you can take.

1. *Know how you procrastinate.* You must recognize the early warning signals and take action before your procrastination ploys take over.

One morning I went to work, opened my planning notebook, and took a look at the day's list. Boy, what a list. I had several major projects—rewrite a brochure, write a newsletter, organize a mailing list of about two thousand names, to list just a few of the tasks. Also, there were some low-priority phone calls I could make if I had time later in the day.

I said to myself, "Let's get these phone calls out of the way; then I can concentrate on the big stuff." In other words, "As soon as I make these calls, then I'll get busy."

Since I admitted my "as soon as" addiction, I am now trained to catch myself every time I utter those words. Then I think objectively about what I'm considering. To say, "As soon as I finish this manuscript, I'll begin accepting speaking engagements," is justifiable. However, to say, "As soon as I think up clever titles for every chapter in my new book, then I'll begin writing the manuscript," is procrastination. Do you see the difference?

Besides "as soon as," some other typical delay tactics are hunger, fatigue, fiddling with low-priority papers, straightening things up, catching up on nonessential jobs, primping, taking breaks, opening mail, and phone calls. ("Oh, hi! Carol? Let's make a date for tennis. How does Friday sound?")

Why do we do it? I wanted to make those low-priority phone calls because they would take little physical effort and I wouldn't have to exert much brainpower. Plus, in just a few minutes I would have had five things crossed off my list. Wow!

Rewriting the brochure, however, would be a grueling process, and what if I messed it up? It was an important job, and failure was a possibility. So I was weighing a guaranteed, easy success against hard work and a chance at failure. I really had to struggle with myself, but I didn't make those calls until later on. (I can still remember how hard that was— turning on the word processor and not reaching for the phone.)

Another reason we putter around with the low pay-off jobs is that they give us instant rewards. With big jobs you don't get that feeling of "Hey! I did it! I'm done!" for days or even weeks, depending on the size of the chore. Small, no-count tasks are here today, gone today, and quickly checked off, and we fool ourselves into thinking that busy-ness and productivity mean the same thing.

Let's face it. We like to act on routine tasks just because they are easy, but they keep us from getting onto the more important things.

Routine is, admittedly, comfortable and seems essential, whereas more important projects are frequently more difficult, unfamiliar, and consequently intimidating. Just as the cure of a disease is facilitated if caught in the early stages of its progression, knowing how you procrastinate gives you a headstart on solving the problem.

2. *Determine when you procrastinate.* Are your drawers filled with half-knitted sweaters, unopened embroidery kits, and yards of fabric purchased with good intentions? Do you have large files of things to be filed? Is the to-do list you made on Monday still good on Friday?

In other words, do you have a hard time getting a project started, and procrastinate at the beginning of a job? Or do you lose steam halfway through and stack up unfinished projects like cannons in a courtyard?

Determine when you procrastinate and, using some of the following ideas, work around your critical point by reinforcing your efforts when you need it most.

3. *Use a planning notebook every day.* Refer to goals you've set, dates, deadlines, appointments, and the running to-do list. (While you're working on your daily list, don't forget to anticipate.)

Simplifying your record keeping will discourage procrastination, and the best way to streamline the process is to use only one calendar. Have you ever been in a group of people and asked someone to tell you what time it was? What happens when two or three people respond? That's right. Everyone has a slightly different answer. "It's 8:10." "Oh, my watch says 8:13." The same holds true for calendars: if you have more than one, you never know which one is accurate and up to date. Also, you're constantly overlapping your efforts, creating more work and more problems for yourself. A family calendar is fine as long as you promise on your word of honor to faithfully coordinate it with your planning notebook.

4. *Break down big jobs.* If it's a big job you're putting off, break it down into a bunch of little tasks. Preferably, each small job should take less than forty-five minutes.

Remember the five afghans I told you I want to make just as soon as I finish this book? That's a big job, but here's how I broke it up:

- Decide what color to make Jeff's afghan.
- Go to yarn shop and choose a pattern.
- Buy yarn.
- Start working.

Each of those tasks will take less than forty-five minutes and would be very manageable. Notice that I'm working on one at a time. Just think how much more complicated it would be to choose colors and patterns for all five at the same time.

Here's how I broke down rewriting the brochure:

- Outline key points in current brochure.
- Delete obsolete material.
- List additional points to include.
- Draw up new, proposed outline.
- Show skeleton draft to boss.
- Rewrite brochure, one section at a time.

If you decided after reading number 2 (deciding when you procrastinate) that you put off *starting* projects, this breaking-down idea is one of the reinforcements you need to use.

Citing the afghan example again, you may argue that breaking up the job as I suggested will involve going to the store for yarn and a pattern five times instead of just doing it once. But for a person who can't get started, choosing five colors and five patterns in one sitting causes the brain to overheat like a $99 Impala, and the task is postponed forever. Simplify the job and you'll start sooner.

5. *Reward yourself.* (This one is perfect for nonfinishers.) What do you have to look forward to when the job is done? What's in it for you? If you haven't done so already, start making that reward list. Will you go to lunch with a friend, take the kids to a drive-in, buy a new suit, or go on a cruise? Whatever reward you choose, make it exciting and attainable.

6. *Involve other people.* (Another good one for nonfinishers.) Tell someone what you plan to do and when you plan to have it completed. (The more people you tell, the better.) Have someone monitor your progress so you'll stay on target. Once you have committed your plans to another person, you not only have your own intrinsic motivation to draw from, but an extrinsic source as well. Thus, when your sizzle starts to fizzle, you'll have that outside power source as a back-up reservoir. It sort of works like a hand on your back, gently pushing you along.

I had a woman in one of my classes who just couldn't wait to set up her planning notebook. Filled with enthusiasm, she went straight home and got started. With a raised eyebrow and deprecating laugh, her husband chided her: "Well, here we go again. You've had more highs and lows than the national weather service. How long do you think *this* program is going to last?"

Instead of exploding in a rage of anger, this woman said, "Okay, you're on. In seven days I want you to ask me how I'm doing with my new system and ask me how many things I've forgotten to do. I'll prove I can do it."

In seven days the man checked back with his wife, and to his surprise, she was still reporting success. "Ah, you're still operating from that rush of motivation you get whenever you go to a lecture," he said. "Let's see how it's going in a month or two."

Well, that's all our friend needed to hear. The challenge worked, and to this day she carries her planning notebook much as a child packs her Cabbage Patch Kid.

Get others involved. It works.

I've already involved you in one of my projects, and you're probably not even aware of it. But someday I may meet you, and you're going to ask me if I ever finished those five afghans. Just knowing I'm going to have to face you someday is what's going to keep me crocheting when I'm halfway through the third one and ready to quit.

7. *Use up odd moments of time.* Continually ask yourself if there is even a small portion of a job you can do now.

8. *Ask, "How long is this really going to take?"* I used to procrastinate changing sheets and emptying the dishwasher until I timed myself and found I can do each job in two minutes. What's the big deal? And what's so hard about a two-minute job? Schuyler always asks me to read her a story at what seems to be the most inconvenient times. How long does it take to read a story? Five minutes, tops. It's nothing to get upset about.

Now, if you discover the job is, in fact, going to take a long time, then break it down until you can handle it.

9. *Hit the golf balls first*. Remember the golf balls a few chapters back? They represent the achievement-oriented tasks we should work on every day. Hit them first! They're usually the most difficult problems you have to deal with, and when you put those things on the back burner, they'll be left for the part of the day when you're the most tired and least motivated. Swing that club and handle the hard things first. That way your self-esteem skyrockets, your productivity soars, and for the rest of the day it's all downhill sledding.

10. *Just start*. Sharpen your pencil, peek out from under the covers, dump one box of garbage in the basement, write the salutation, put on your running shoes. Do something *now*. One thing usually leads to another.

Years ago we had a wonderful neighbor, George Merrill. He was the busiest and most organized man on the planet. He had an ordinary two-car garage that was always in such perfect order you could easily make a U-turn in it with your car. His wife, Carma, once told me that he could even find his socks in the dark and get the right color.

I was impressed, but I must admit to a little skepticism. "Maybe he only has black socks," I said to myself. So, curious as I am, I decided to pay more attention to George. Whenever he was outside working on his immaculately groomed yard, I would peek out the window and check out his socks. Brown, blue, black, white. Somehow I wasn't surprised. Finally I had had enough. "George," I said, "how do you do it? You are so busy. How do you stay so organized? What's your secret?"

I'll always be grateful to George Merrill for sharing his secret with me. He said simply, "Do it. Do it right. Do it right now." Then he added, "If you don't have time to do it right, when will you have time to do it over?"

What words of wisdom! Now, thanks to a thoughtful friend, I have "Do it—Do it right—Do it right now" done up in a cross-stitch sampler in my living room. It serves as a constant reminder that I (one who needs frequent jump-starting) must start and do something now.

There you have it—ten antidotes for procrastination.

1. Know how you procrastinate.
2. Determine when you procrastinate.
3. Use a planning notebook every day.
4. Break down big jobs.
5. Reward yourself.
6. Involve other people.
7. Use up odd moments of time.
8. Ask, "How long is this really going to take?"
9. Hit the golf balls first.
10. Just start.

That's all well and good, but knowledge and intention are weak motivators. You must actually put these ideas into practice if you want to see success. Each of these ten points is a specific method to use when you need to get yourself motivated. Each of them works!

Remember, it is very difficult to change your mood by a sheer act of will. It is much easier to change your behavior— but changing your behavior will, in turn, change your mood. Act yourself into feeling different. Don't wait until your mood changes. Change your behavior now, and your mood will follow along.

That's why number 10—"Just start"—is such an effective motivator. It changes your behavior. Here's an example:

More times than I care to admit, I've stared at the word *exercise* on my daily to-do list and thought, "Oh, yuk! I don't want to exercise. I am too tired to exercise. I won't exercise." Then I remember that my behavior can change my mood. "Okay, here's the deal," I say to myself. "Just put the aerobics tape in the VCR, turn it on, and watch it for a few minutes. If you still can't make yourself exercise, turn off the TV." So I change my behavior and turn on the tape. That one simple act almost always changes my mood, and I'm up and moving around.

Keep your mood in check in the first place by getting mentally prepared. Planning at night before bed, I mentally prepare for what's coming up the next day. Driving to work, I think about how I'm going to handle an irate customer. Sitting behind my desk about midafternoon, I start reminding myself that I need to tackle the laundry as soon as I get home. Mental preparedness is one way to keep a bad or lethargic mood from getting a stronghold on your behavior.

What if you're really unmotivated and for some reason you can't even take the first step? And what if getting yourself mentally prepared doesn't do the trick? What then?

I've had days like that, days when you look at the list of things you have to do and just can't seem to earn a check mark for even the simplest, most fundamental task. What do I do? I flip to the running to-do list in my planning notebook and read the entire page. Then I ask myself if there is anything on that list I could talk myself into doing. Usually, there's at least one job that sounds remotely interesting. (Return Carol's cake pan, order business cards, pick up a replacement bulb for the slide projector, find a good recipe for Shrimp Scampi, add pictures to the photo album.) It may not be on today's list, but at least I'm doing something. Besides, I intended to do it sooner or later anyway.

Try it yourself. After you've finished that odd job, you'll run head on into the best motivator of all—success! You finished something! You did it! Maybe *now* you can face that to-do list.

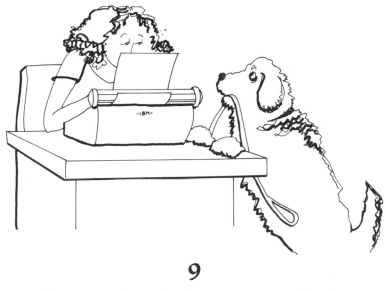

9

Interrupting the Interruption Cycle

How to Control Interruptions

Pose this question to one thousand women and they'll each give you the same answer: "What is your biggest time waster?" Procrastination? No. Lack of self-discipline? No. Unrealistic time estimates? No. Unhesitatingly, they'd pick interruptions, hands—or should I say thumbs—down!

Various studies have shown that managers are interrupted approximately every eight minutes. As a mom, I'd say the same holds true at home too, although that estimate may be a little conservative.

"I want a drink of water." "Please comb Barbie and Skipper's hair." "Where's my other shoe?" Answer the phone. Rescue the baby from the edge of the stairs. Walk the dog. Answer the doorbell. Tote that barge, lift that bale. Yes, interruptions are the bane of motherhood.

But be advised: Interruptions are not created equal. There are two types of interruptions, those that are necessary and those that are unnecessary.

1. *Necessary interruptions.*

Yes, some interruptions *are* necessary. For example, if your children never interrupted you, they could die. "Mom, the baby is in the street." "Excuse, me, Mother, but the house is on fire." "Oh, Mom, there's a rattlesnake in the backyard." I repeat, some interruptions are necessary.

Still others, while not life threatening, are also necessary. The end of the wash cycle signals it's time to put the clothes into the dryer. Your boss delegates a "stop all the presses, here's a high priority job that must be done now" project. The school calls to say one of your kids has the chickenpox. A friend is going through a crisis and she calls to say, "I need you. Can you come over?"

Just realizing that many interruptions are important and necessary should help you to cope with their dogged demands. However, there are others, which leads me to

2. *Unnecessary interruptions.*

Any interruption you could have planned for or prevented is an unnecessary interruption. These are the hidden destroyers, so to speak, because they're often masked by seeming urgencies and sometimes appear necessary.

Imagine that it's ten below zero outside and the winds are howling, and your son asks where his gloves are. Now, that may seem like a necessary interruption because, due to the weather conditions, he desperately needs to wear his gloves to school. But think again. If the gloves had a specific place where they belonged and had been put back in that spot, you would not have been interrupted.

Here's another scenario. The brakes go out in the car and it's simply unsafe to drive it another mile. The brakes must be fixed today. Necessary or unnecessary? Unnecessary. Yes, the brakes must be fixed, but usually you can sense when the brakes are on their way out days before they grind down to their last screeching halt. The brake job could have been planned for another day. It was simply procrastination that caused today's interruption.

It's Saturday morning and you're anxious to tackle several projects you've been waiting to get to all week. About halfway through cleaning the closets, your husband announces (with the enthusiasm and excitement of a man whose team has just won the Super Bowl), "Come outside and help me. I decided today would be a great day to sod the front yard. They're delivering the grass right now!"

Necessary or unnecessary? Unnecessary. Now, hear me out. I'm not advocating divorce court. First, something as major as sodding the front yard should have been planned in advance (although in this case, you weren't included in those plans).

Here's another example of how anticipation eliminates untimely interruptions: Suppose on Friday night you tell your husband (or any other time offender) what you are planning to do on Saturday. Tell him you've been meaning to get these projects out of the way for a long time. "Can you think of anything that will keep me from my schedule?"

If he says, "Yes. I wanted to sod the front yard tomorrow," you can negotiate a compromise or offer to fix lunch for his friends who could come to help him. If he says, "No," then you're off and running.

Here's my typical approach: "Jim, this is what I've planned to do next Saturday. If you have something scheduled that needs my attention, will you let me know today?"

One of the biggest problems couples have is communicating. You fill your own head with ideas, dreams, and plans—and he does the same. Then you wake up one morning and decide this is the day you'll carry out those plans—and he does the same. And guess what? Pretty soon somebody's plans start to look more like a hubcap spinning for the gutter. So think, plan, and dream *out loud*. The other person in your life cannot read your mind. Anticipate and communicate to eliminate unnecessary interruptions and dashed hopes.

Anticipate interruptions from the kids, too. I can set my watch by Schuyler's schedule. Every weekday morning at 10:30 A.M. sharp she comes to me with slumped shoulders and sighs, "It's abysmal time"—meaning there's nothing good to watch on TV. Knowing this interruption is coming, I can plan something and prepare for it: invite a friend to come over, read to her, or suggest other activities for her to do.

Generally, I just take her interruptions in stride. But once in a while I desperately need to have a span of time when I'm not interrupted, like when I'm putting the final touches on a dinner party, doing a long-distance radio interview, making "I Can Do It" certificates for every child in the elementary school, or wallpapering the bathroom.

When I genuinely need some whole-hearted cooperation, I reach into my bag of tricks—which is also handy when someone's stuck in bed with the flu (and bored to death), or when we're waiting for an hour in the doctor's office. So, what's in that magical bag? Here's a peek.

1. We subscribe to a few children's magazines. Before the children have a chance to read them, I photocopy some of the activity pages (such as mazes, "what's wrong with this picture," word searches, "find 14 things that begin with the letter B," and hidden pictures) and keep them stockpiled in a file folder. The kids enjoy the magazines and use the activity pages, but months (sometimes years) later when I need to keep them busy, I pull out an activity page from the file and it's as effective and fresh as it was the first time they saw it.

2. To make a bubble-blowing solution, use 1 quart of water and 1/4 cup of Joy dishwashing liquid. (That particular brand works best, for some reason.) Straws and funnels make good bubble blowers.

3. Here's my favorite play dough recipe: Combine 1 cup flour, 1 cup water, 1/2 cup salt, 2 tablespoons oil, and 2 teaspoons cream of tartar. Add a few drops of food coloring, if desired. Cook mixture over low heat until it forms a ball in the middle of the pan. Drop ball of dough onto a

breadboard and knead until cooled. Store dough in tightly covered container or plastic bag.

4. Older children might enjoy sculpting and painting their creations. Here's a recipe for a dough that hardens and can be painted: Mix together 4 cups flour, 1 cup salt, and 1½ cups water; knead until smooth. Sculpt and mold as desired. Bake sculpted items at 350 degrees for about an hour, or until slightly browned. Paint the cooled creation with tempera paints.

5. Present the child with a small box containing some old magazines or catalogs, some scissors, construction paper, and a glue stick (or muselage glue with a rubber-tipped applicator, or a plastic tube of roll-on water glue). If you're not afraid of a mess, toss in a small container of glitter.

6. Schuyler entertains herself for hours on end playing dress-up and making up her face with cornstarch powder and lip gloss.

7. If you haven't any glamorous cast-offs the kids can use as dress-up clothes, a secondhand store is the place to stock up. An evening gown, jewelry, even fake furs, can be purchased for very little money. (I spent half my childhood playing Miss America.)

8. Our boys have kept themselves busy with a block of wood, a hammer, and a box of nails. Or we can give them a screwdriver and let them disassemble a broken stereo, clock, electronic game, or tape recorder. We won't hear a peep out of them for at least an hour. (One of our children even built a battery-operated robot out of a cardboard box and some old electrical parts.)

9. Styrofoam packing forms are also fun for the kids to play with. They use them as army forts (G.I. Joe headquarters) or Barbie apartments, and they cut them into chunks to make furniture or other creations.

10. Save small boxes and scraps of fabric so the kids can make doll furniture and clothes. The boys, of course, will use the fabric as bandages when G.I. Joe gets injured in the

line of duty—and if Joe doesn't pull through, the fabric will be there to turn him into a mummy.

11. Save the hundreds of magazines stickers you get in the mail and pull them out for a child to lick and stick on a piece of paper.

12. Save the trinkets that come in cereal boxes and use them as new toys when you need to keep a child occupied.

13. Buy four or five storybooks and record them on a tape recorder, ringing a bell as a signal to turn the page. Using the alias "Ding Dong Mama," I've relied on this one a lot, and our kids play the tapes until they wear out.

14. Let the kids make jewelry using string (shoelaces, or shoestring licorice), O-shaped cereal, cut-up straws, and macaroni.

15. A bowl of marshmallows, gumdrops, and jelly beans and a box of round toothpicks keep the children busy building creations they can eat.

16. Paste a coloring-book picture on a small piece of poster board and, using a paper punch, punch holes around the perimeter. The child then colors the picture and "frames" it by sewing through the holes with a length of colorful yarn.

17. Teach the children how to make a wax picture. Color a design on a piece of paper using any color but black. Be sure the entire sheet of paper is covered with color. Then color with black crayon over the entire design. Next, using a dried-up ballpoint pen (or a straightened paper clip), scratch a design in the black crayon to expose the bright colors beneath.

18. Rent a video, or present the child with a few new puzzles, a sticker book, or paper dolls. Anything new usually holds a child's attention—at least for a while. And that's all you want, a little time for yourself, time that's uninterrupted.

Satisfied needs are not motivators, so these activities should be used infrequently enough that they retain their allure. For example, our children have a large covered container of cracked wheat (cornmeal also works well) that I let them play with. They dump the wheat into a few large cake pans and use them as miniature sandboxes. (Sure, it's a little messy, but it's clean and easy to sweep up.) I let the kids play with wheat only about once every three months or so; used only that occasionally, it's always an attention grabber and keeps them entertained for quite a while.

One last anticipation technique is to fill the kids up. Here's what I mean: If you know you're going to be preoccupied with a project for the next little while, satisfy the kids' hunger for your attention before you get started. Read a few stories to them, set out a few snacks for them to help themselves, play a game, sing, or work on a simple art project together. Satisfied in this way, they won't feel so neglected when you get busy.

Yes, the kids are going to interrupt you, but if you fill them up first or have some diversion activities ready, you'll not only eliminate a bunch of interruptions, but both you and the kids will also be a lot happier.

Now for the humdinger. There is yet another type of unnecessary interruption, and a conquest of this is comparable to David defeating Goliath. These are interruptions you seek out. Whenever I'm doing something difficult (like writing this book), or unpleasant (like washing the windows), or tedious (like filing tax returns), my head says I don't want to be interrupted—but in my heart I'm suffering withdrawal symptoms. I *need* an interruption. If Jim says, "Come on and ride into town with me," I'm in the car with my seat belt fastened before he can even comb his hair or button his shirt.

Or a friend will call on the phone and my alter ego Chatty Cathy takes over. And when my friend says, "I'll let you go, I know you're busy," I counter with, "Me busy? I'm not doing a thing!"

Or I'll get up and go into a co-worker's office under the guise of needing to ask her a legitimate question. Of course, I'm hoping the inquiry will grow into a full-blown conversation, the subject of which doesn't matter in the slightest.

Determining self-induced interruptions requires painstaking self-honesty. These insidious interrupters may just be one of the methods you use to procrastinate an important task. Once you know that you're sometimes at fault, you can catch yourself before the time has been needlessly wasted.

Here's the pep talk my head gives to my heart whenever I encounter those vulnerable moments: "You're an easy target right now. You don't really want to be doing this job, so beware. You may come up with a lot of creative ways to put it off. Be on guard. Watch for any sign of mutiny."

Lest you be too hard on yourself, it is perfectly acceptable to take a break now and then. I only offer this advice. Consider the part self-interruption plays in your life, and every time your will starts to flicker, ask yourself, "Do I really need a break, or am I just looking for a diversion?"

There is one other large cross section of women who, collectively, are extremely tough on themselves. They function as if they're strapped to jetpacks soaring from one activity to another, yet they feel their efforts are in vain. They wonder what to do about their incessant time demands. And who are the members of this indefatigable group? They are women with young children.

If this describes you, take heart. There's a very good reason why you feel frustrated. Almost every interruption caused by a child under approximately three years of age is necessary! So if you're a mom with a young child, or two, or three, you must be a master at eliminating unnecessary interruptions from your life in order to get the most from your time. Constantly remind yourself that you're doing everything humanly possible. Remember, this is motherhood. These interruptions are necessary. Besides, they won't last forever. It just seems like it.

As a matter of fact, while I was writing the last one hundred words, my little daughter interrupted me three times. She was watching Captain Kangaroo and the color on the TV went out (heaven forbid), so I had to fine-tune the television set. (Necessary, sort of.) Next, she had to make a trip to the bathroom. (Necessary.) Then she couldn't find one of her favorite toys and needed me to help with the search-and-rescue mission. (Unnecessary.)

Guess which interruption kept me from working for the greatest length of time? Of course, the unnecessary one. Had I followed my own rule to have things put back where they belong every day, Mr. Potato Head would not have been a missing person and no search posse would have been organized.

Here's a great technique to help you get a handle on your interruptions once and for all. About now, corporate time-management experts would recommend that you keep a time log and record every fifteen minutes how you've been spending your time. Oh sure. You're already interrupted every five to eight minutes anyway. Now you have to interrupt yourself every fifteen minutes on top of that? Never. That's exactly why most women don't keep time logs.

I'm going to suggest something very effective and far less demanding. All you have to do is make your daily action list and proceed as usual. (So far, so good. You have to make the list anyway.) Then, when something comes along to distract you or when something keeps you from pursuing today's direction, make a note in your planning notebook on today's calendar page.

It was this very exercise that proved to me how many interruptions I was seeking out. In just a few days I had such things on my interruption list as these: Went to the mall. (This appeared three times.) Went out to lunch. Rode to the city with Jim. Picked up videos.

I hear you. "What's wrong with a little spontaneity?" "Are you telling me I can't go out to lunch anymore, or go to the mall?" "You're taking all the fun out of life." Whoa!

Certainly there's nothing wrong with doing any of the items on that interruption list. But remember, this exercise is to help you compare how you plan to spend your time with

what you actually do. And if interruptions are seriously affecting your ability to function, then you must discover the source
of those interruptions.

Before I realized *I* was the enemy, I was pointing that old
finger of blame again—at my husband, at our children, and
at my boss. But *I* was causing most of my own problems.
Me. I was the culprit.

Of course, there were other interruptions on the lists. A
few, I noticed, were constant and recurring. One son, ten
years old, was always interrupting me when he needed his
hair combed. Another boy was always thirsty for a glass of
milk but was too small to handle a gallon jug. Thus, I had to
continually stop what I was doing to comb hair and pour
milk. *Ah-ha*, I thought. *I can prevent these unnecessary
interruptions!* I taught Steven how to comb his hair, and
kept covered glasses of milk in the refrigerator for Jeffrey.

Other items indicated that Jim was dumping a lot of his
procrastinated jobs on me. Naturally, these chores had been
neglected long enough that they had become both urgent and
necessary (car brakes, car inspections, check deposits, and so
forth). So, using anticipation and communication, I've been
able to plan more effectively and eliminate many of those
interruptions.

At last I have more time for spontaneity—guilt-free spontaneity at that. But I do try to weigh priorities so that those
things which are most important are accomplished first. I
always remember that too much careless abandon, too much
spontaneity, is what got me into trouble in the first place.

Try this exercise. It really won't hurt a bit. And if you
don't want to be chained to your planning notebook all day,
keep an index card and pencil in your pocket to make notes.
If you get to the end of the day and realize you didn't record
one interruption, sit down and look at your day's to-do list.
What jobs were left uncompleted? Note why you didn't get
to them. Jot down any interruptions or other deviations you
can think of that occurred during the day. No, you won't

remember every little interruption, but you'll get a broad idea of how you spent your time.

You cannot begin to control your interruptions until you're specifically aware of them. We all know that we're interrupted incessantly, but until we know why, when, and by whom, we can't control the interruptions or eliminate the unnecessary ones.

Whenever you incur an interruption, ask yourself if it is necessary or unnecessary. Could you have anticipated and prevented it? Or did you seek it out or secretly welcome it? Be brutally honest with yourself, and you'll see interruptions drop in priority as your biggest time waster.

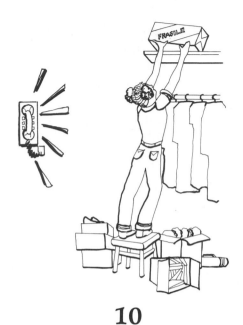

10

Here's Your Hat—What's Your Hurry?

Controlling the Phone and Visitors

No discussion of interruptions would be complete, I suppose, without giving consideration to the telephone. The phone, I dare say, has brought out the beast in me on numerous occasions.

Here I am cleaning the front hall closet. While sitting knee deep on all fours surrounded by a bowling ball, two tennis rackets, a bait bucket, a tackle box, the vacuum cleaner, four dirty sweatshirts, a few unmatched socks, three ski boots, a thermos jug, a Creative Stitchery kit, a furnace filter, a couple of empty shoe boxes, and Mr. Potato Head, the phone rings. Untying my legs, I look for a weak spot in the pile where I can break through. Four rings, three bruises, a wrenched back, and two chipped nails later I pick up the impatient receiver.

"Hello. This is Conrad the Computer. We at Cameraland hope you are having a nice day. We are . . ." Click. "I was having a nice day before you interrupted me, Conrad," I fume.

Now wait a minute. It wasn't completely Conrad's fault. After all, is it against the law to let the phone ring? No, but that takes some self-discipline.

Think about your phone calls. When was the last time you received a call that was so important it couldn't wait until later? Personally, I haven't had one of those for over a year. Most of the calls we receive are not urgent and don't need to be handled now, but for some reason we risk life, limb, and the pursuit of happiness just to uncover the mystery. Who is it? What do they want?

Put yourself out of your misery. When you're too busy to answer the phone, unplug it, or turn on the answering machine.

But what if the school should call? Every school has a back-up number to call in case of emergency when the parents or legal guardians of the child can't be reached. If your back-up person lives close by, call her and say, "I'm unplugging the phone for an hour. If the school calls, come and get me, I'll be home."

Although telephone answering machines are scorned by many, they do provide a worthwhile service and keep you from being unnecessarily interrupted. With their popularity increasing, I've become more and more comfortable talking into an answering machine. I also enjoy the added reassurance that I'm not interrupting anyone. In certain parts of the country answering machines are a way of life. Not only is there a chicken in every pot, but there's a machine by every phone.

Here are some other alternatives. Have your children answer the phone and take messages for you if you're busy. Don't worry about offending someone. I would rather leave a message than interrupt someone who's soaking in a hot bath.

If it's a telephone solicitor, the Better Business Bureau suggests that you ask the soliciting company to state its request in writing and to mail the information to you. One of my friends always responds by saying, "I'm sorry. I never buy (or subscribe to) things over the phone."

To get your name removed from or added to national telephone-solicitation lists, contact the Telephone Preference Service, 6 East 43rd Street, New York, New York 10017. Include your name, address, and phone number (including area code). Be sure to state whether you want to be added to or removed from the lists.

This may not keep local businesses from contacting you, but perhaps you'll eliminate some magazine subscription drives. You know, the ones that offer you five magazines a week and you pay only the shipping and handling charges. Translation: You get five magazines a month (four of which you have no use for) and they only cost you $124.28 a year. Such a deal.

Suppose the caller is a real live person, an acquaintance, a friend, and there's no time to visit. For heaven's sake, if the caller is polite enough to ask, "Have you got a minute?" or "Are you busy?"—be honest.

"I'm shampooing the carpet but I'm never too busy for you. What can I do for you?"

But what if the friend wants to chat and you're on your way out the front door! Just say simply and honestly, "I can't talk now. When is a good time for me to call you back?"

We women have a tremendous fear of offending, and that's a noble quality, but honesty is also important and will be appreciated by true friends. And do you know what I've discovered? It's only difficult to say, "I can't talk now" or "I've got to run" the first few times. Sure, you'll be scared and nervous, but as you do it, it'll become easier and more natural.

Another thing to consider is that *you* are sometimes the interrupter. Treat others with the same courtesy you'd like to receive. "Are you busy?" "Can you talk or do you want me to call you back later?" "Is this a bad time?" When you're calling someone for a particular reason, get to the point. The other party will appreciate it.

One Christmas I was the neighborhood chairman in charge of rounding up Christmas gifts for a needy family in our area. Basically, all I had to do was call all my neighbors and ask for donations. I'll never forget the warm response I got from one expert time manager.

"Hi, Joann. This is Deniece. I'm in charge of the sub-for-Santa project this year." At that point Joann interrupted me and said, "Great! What can I do to help?" I have never forgotten that conversation, though it occurred seven or eight years ago. She valued her time and she valued mine, yet she was eager to help me and I truly felt the warmth of her charity. What can I do for you? How can I help? What do you need? All are sincere, caring words that help you to get to the point of the conversation.

If you're visiting with someone in person and you must call time on the visit, again, use good manners. Look at your watch while you're talking, interrupt yourself, and say, "I've got to get going." Finish your sentence and say your good-byes. If you and the other person are sitting, stand up only when *you* are talking.

Here's one last tip for dodging interruptions: If it's possible, schedule some quiet time for yourself. If you're working, try to squeeze in at least one quiet time session a week.

One friend of ours is a virtuoso at the piano and requires of herself one hour of uninterrupted practice every day. She prepares lunch for her boys, turns on *Sesame Street,* and sits down at the piano. She has taught the children not to leave the family room or to interrupt her unless it's an emergency.

Another friend hires a babysitter to watch her children so she can go to her study to work on a novel she's writing. The children are safe and well attended to at home, and Mom's right nearby.

I have two friends who signed up for art and sewing classes. Neither woman actually needs art or sewing lessons because they're both experts, but the classes give them structured and uninterrupted time to enjoy their skills. An added plus: the mess is contained in a school building four miles away from home!

Another way to grab a few minutes of peace is to use naptime. A child's nap is the glue that holds a mother together, so take advantage of it. As soon as the child goes down for a nap, stop whatever you're doing and begin your quiet-time activity. When the child awakens, get back to whatever you were doing before he or she went to sleep.

Maybe a more insouciant approach would work. When I wrote my third book, Schuyler was two and a half years old, so I spent most of my time at the library to remove myself from her necessary interruptions. She was left in the care of her father or her brothers and wasn't too disturbed by my absence, yet she still remembers it.

This time (she's four now) I just reasoned with her. "Schuy, Mom's working on another book and I need your help. Can you leave me alone for a while? If you really need something, come and get me, okay? Otherwise, I'll have to go back to the library to work on the book."

She's old enough now to understand my reasoning and to entertain herself. Every so often she comes in for a reassuring hug, or she wants me to rock one of her babies to sleep, but basically she's been very cooperative.

Actually, the library is a great place to get away. It's quiet and peaceful, and you can take the kids with you. Take them to story hour, and while they're being entertained, relax and enjoy yourself.

The car is another hideout that's often overlooked, though it's pretty much a fair-weather friend. Reading, writing, thinking, paperwork, job-related projects, crafts—many things can be performed in the quiet solitude of your car. (This idea is very beneficial to a person whose job involves frequent interruptions.)

Also, for the working woman who needs to get away for a quiet block of time, look for an unused office or conference room. Is there a small restaurant or snack shop close to your office? If so, occupy one of the nethermost tables while you outline a report, write a rough draft, or organize a sales territory.

Interruptions have the unprecedented power to kill your whole day, yet by controlling them you can easily save two hours! Won't you try some of these ideas? With a little thought and some imagination, you'll quickly discover solutions that work well for you.

11

Pulling the Plug

Learn to Tame the TV

"Krystle fears Blake has fallen in love with Alexis again; Amanda disappears; Leslie Carrington meets Adam and her old friend Dex."

"Dave fails the bar exam and hits rock bottom; a woman must decide between a young man in love with her or someone her own age."

"A family's backyard becomes a battleground for hungry little creatures and the human-looking bounty hunters pursuing them."

And for this we become purely passive spectators, warm bodies to be subjected to a series of emotions, objects to be worked on. We position our chairs, gobble down bags of Cheetos and pounds of popcorn, and before long all that Cosby Show spirit has settled firmly about the hips.

Families separate into groups cloistered around different TV sets so as not to miss a favorite program. Channel zappers flip feverishly from one station to the next, avoiding commercials and searching for something more interesting.

A barrage of advertisements make us (and especially our children) think we don't have all the things we should have—that we don't have all the things we *need!* But the bottom line is that every time we plop down in front of the tube, we're substituting a slice of our lives for the sake of a superstation.

Yes, I watch television. And sometimes I sit there vegetating and enjoy every minute of it. But I've been an addict, and I had to learn how to keep TV watching within reasonable parameters. With only one child and a small house to care for, I turned to the television to absorb empty, unfulfilled hours. I became a game-show zealot. I would freeze in a state of suspended animation waiting to see if contestant number one would choose door number two on "Let's Make a Deal." I gasped in horror as the reigning champ risked it all and lost it on "Jeopardy." I shouted answers to unknowing contestants on "Password." The seemingly innocent viewing of one soap opera led to the destruction of entire afternoons as the cliff-hanging conclusion of one show spilled into another's gripping plot.

I'll never forget one afternoon when I was perched in my usual spot, staring with prolonged passionate interest at the scene unfolding before my eyes. Our little boy, then two and a half, said, "Is that the mean grandma?"

Though I quickly answered, "Yes," that one piercing question was so thought-provoking that I couldn't dismiss it from my mind. That grandma *was* mean. She was evil and nasty, and I asked myself, Would I invite that woman over for dinner? Would I want her anywhere near my precious little boy? Certainly not. Yet, I was doing just that every day. Every time I touched the dial I was welcoming the mean grandma and her equally disgusting cohorts into our living room. I was allowing the motley bunch to associate with my son.

That was all it took. I went cold turkey—no more soap operas from that day on.

Game shows, though, were harmless, I thought, so I threw myself into them with even more fervor. Then I gradually realized I was making out of my life a wasteland of human potential. The hours in front of the TV were keeping me from those achievement-oriented tasks so vital to a happy, fulfilling life. Golden moments to teach and play with our children were squandered. I needed a major TV-time budget cut.

Perhaps you're not as far gone as I was. (And if you're working, certainly you don't have time to be!) Maybe you're just worried about the effects television is having on your family. Regardless of the role TV plays in your life, if you're interested in loosening its grasp, here are a few ways to tame the tube.

1. Decide objectively and in advance what programs you're going to watch. If you change channels the way the afore-mentioned Alexis changes clothes (which is to say often), you're going to be sucked into whatever comes along. So decide what you will watch; then, when your selected show is over, turn off the TV or leave the room if others are still watching.

Television producers know how to attract viewers. Just before the program airs they often show what's called a teaser, which is meant to pique your interest so you'll stay tuned. Another ploy is to postpone the first commercial for fifteen or twenty minutes so you'll be hooked into the plot, wanting to see who does what to whom and how. Don't tempt yourself. Just get up and turn off the set before you're suckered into watching something else.

2. Don't get involved with all of the new series offered at the beginning of the new TV season in the fall. You'll never miss what you've never seen.

3. Get up during the commercials and do something else. Unload the dishwasher, water the plants, vacuum the carpet, read an article, or write a thank-you note.

4. If you're a game-show-aholic, you need to know that only a fraction of the time the show is on the air is actually spent playing the game. The bulk of the time is spent joking with guests and touting products that are given as prizes. Decide that you'll watch the game show only on certain days. Or tune in only for the fast-money round, the big deal, the bonus minute. That way, you'll get to enjoy the thrill of victory or, more likely, the agony of defeat. In other words, you'll feel the show's excitement without having to put in a thirty-minute time investment.

5. Soap operas are extremely addictive and consequently hard to forestall. But the action moves so slowly that you can keep up the gist of the story by watching only once or twice a month. If you must keep up with the story line, read about the plot in a soap-opera magazine or ask a friend who's also hooked.

A friend of ours who is a schoolteacher has kept up with one soap opera for eight years just by talking to parents at parent-teacher conferences. Allowing for occasional preempting, I figure this teacher has saved herself about 250 hours a year (a little more than ten days). Over a period of eight years she has accrued nearly three solid months of time.

6. Leave the house. Go shopping, attend a concert, sign up for a lecture series, work out, visit a friend. (This is a good diversion if you're trying to withdraw from soap operas.) Find something more interesting to do. Check your reward list and the running to-do list. Is there something on either list that sounds more stimulating and interesting than the program you're contemplating?

7. Don't plan your routine around what's on TV. Meals, activities, appointments, and the kids' bedtimes should be established first. Then, if there's time for a program or two, work it in around your schedule.

8. Go on a TV fast. Decide on a time period when you'll do without television—a day, a weekend, a week, or longer. Experiment with new activities, and you may discover new interests and talents.

9. Turn off the TV when no one is watching. (If you just have it on for noise, turn on the stereo or the radio instead.) Television is so seductive that it will lure you to it unawares. So turn it (and the temptation) off!

Experts agree that when used wisely and in moderation, TV can be an excellent learning tool. In addition, there are programs that do provide wonderful entertainment. The key, though, is moderation, and if you feel you're tipping the scale toward excess, start today and Tame That Tube. (Great name for a game show, don't you think?)

12

Home Sweat Home

Setting Priorities in Your Housework

If I were rummaging through your husband's closet, could I find a pair of bell-bottom pants, a tie-dyed shirt, or a Nehru jacket? And what about *your* closet. Would I discover three sets of clothes? (You know, the clothes you're wearing now, the ones you plan to wear when you lose weight, and the outfits you're hanging on to just in case they come back in style.)

Would you rather have your gums scraped than enter your kids' bedrooms, the basement, or the garage? Do you sometimes stash hoards of stuff in cupboards, closets, or drawers just to get them out of sight? Do you collapse in a heap every night and wonder where the day went?

If you do, you have plenty of company. With family, social, community, and church responsibilities pulling you in a hundred different directions (and perhaps a job creating even more demands on your time and energy), it's understandable if you feel overwhelmed. But you can take control of your life and put an end to the time wasters that are responsible for what may amount to the grand larceny of your life.

"And what," you may ask, "does a Nehru jacket or a tie-dyed shirt have to do with time management?"

Good question. If you think about it for a minute, you'll realize that most of your time is spent managing things: dishes, laundry, trash, paperwork, bathtub ring, appointments, lessons, hobbies, dust, food, and so on. It only follows, then, that the more effectively you manage these physical things, the more time you have to pursue your chosen activities.

Let's take a minute to discover which homemaking tasks affect your time if they're neglected. I've given this subject a lot of thought because as a working mother myself, I've had to eliminate a lot of housecleaning fluff from my life (such as dusting the water heater weekly, washing windows six times a year, spring and fall housecleaning, and mopping the kitchen floor every day). I soon learned that order is more important than clean, at least as far as time is concerned.

Is your time affected if the dusting is left undone? No. What about vacuuming or bedmaking? No. Windows, walls, or woodwork scrubbed? No. But let the laundry go for a few weeks, and your time starts to go up in smoke. You either wear what you wore yesterday or run to the laundry room to wash what you need. Multiply that by the number of people in your household and you're out of control fast.

You'll have an instant replay of the melee if you let the house go for a week or so without picking things up and putting them away. Likewise if meals are accidentally produced. With the latter, small children unnecessarily interrupt you for food and older family members prepare snacks for themselves, creating individual messes and further infringing upon your time.

Now, I'm not proposing that you let the cleaning go until you hear from the health department, but priorities are vitally important, especially if you're working (for money, that is), if you have lots of preschoolers, or if you're struggling with a health problem or some other extraordinary demand. The cold, hard fact is that if you have lots of demands on your time, the cost is usually found by settling for less with your homemaking. There's no such thing as having it all.

So, what are the priorities? Here they are in order of importance:

- Pick up the house every day. (Three times a week, minimum.)
- Keep the laundry current. (Once a week, minimum.)
- Plan and serve nutritious meals every day.
- Keep the kitchen clean.
- Keep the bathroom(s) clean.
- (Optional) Keep the entry way attractive and neat.

In the NCAA basketball championship tournament is an elite group known as the Final Four. In housework we have what's know as the Big Three: picking up, laundry, and meals. When I really have my back up against a wall and time is impossible to come by (say, for example, when I'm nearing a book deadline, I've just had a baby, or some major crisis hits), I worry only about the Big Three. Everything else sort of gets a lick and a promise. I am always amazed how smoothly things run even when only those three things are done. Let's spend a few minutes on each of these priorities to help you gather the information you may need to conquer them once and for all.

1. *Pick up the house every day.*

One of the best reasons for organizing cupboards, closets, and drawers is to make picking up easier and faster. Have you ever noticed what a mess people make when they're looking for something? Do you avoid putting something away because the drawer or closet it belongs in is jumbled and messy? Having an underlying sense of order prevents all that.

A neat, orderly work place is an invitation to get busy, whereas a hodgepodge of junk, debris, and half-finished projects stifles enthusiasm and promotes delay, diversion, and procrastination.

When I first got things organized, I decided that I was probably the only one in the family who really cared. Thus, I knew I would be the one who had to keep all systems working. Whenever I opened a closet, cupboard, or drawer and noticed something out of place, I spent a few seconds putting it back in its designated spot. All I was doing was maintaining and protecting my initial time investment.

Have you ever lost ten pounds and gained back fifteen? Have you ever spent hours exercising over a period of months, only to stop when the bad weather hit? Sure, we all have. And what a waste it is to let that initial investment slip through your fingers for lack of one simple procedure: maintenance.

If you want to be the winner (and the prize is free time), you have to pay the price. You cannot be a martyr about this. You cannot scream, nag, or demand cooperation. Silently, and in good spirits, carry out your plan. Once everyone begins to notice the change in the family mood and atmosphere, they'll feel more cooperative. In addition they will know exactly where things belong, and their help will be more effective. Now imagine how fast things can be picked up and put away when everything down to the tiniest screw has a specific place. It takes a fraction of the time it would take otherwise.

Years ago when all of our children were little, my sister and I used to get together once in a while so all the cousins could spend a day playing together. And what a time they had! Every toy in the house was strewn through every room, giving the effect of a simulated explosion at the North Pole.

When the day was spent, Judy would always insist that her kids help us clean up the mess, but I always refused their help. Dumb, you say? Not really. My children knew the system. They knew which dishpan the Legos went in, which container held the G.I. Joes, and which basket the small vehicles belonged in. One or two of the children were in charge of rounding things up, and the rest of us quickly tossed the toys in their respective bins. I always assured Judy that it took only a few minutes—and it did, five minutes tops. Could you put away every toy in your house in five minutes? That's why order and organization—a system—are so important to the picking-up process.

I have another goal I try hard to maintain, though I'm not always successful. That is to put everything in the house exactly where it belongs at least once a day. I can't admit to doing that every single day, but I do it several times a week. I've learned that less than three times a week is courting disaster, and then you start wasting unnecessary amounts of time.

The nicest gift I give myself is when we pick up the house before going to bed. I sleep better, get out of bed easier (and that in itself is a miracle), and have a head start on the day.

Pick up! It's the most important thing you can do to save time.

2. *Keep the laundry current.*

Laundry is one of those jobs that's never finished. As soon as you empty the hamper, someone tosses in a towel, a pair of denim jeans, belts, shoes, you name it. That's why a laundry schedule is so important. With a schedule, *you* are finished. Sure, in the meantime things may be piling up, but Monday's wash is completed. "I'm done. I don't have to worry about the laundry until Wednesday." That statement always gives me a sense of accomplishment and completion, two sensations we homemakers experience infrequently. Sticking to a schedule, though, can make you feel like that all the time.

When doing the laundry spans the course of more than one day, you're always on the defense, just trying to catch up. It's a miserable feeling. There's a heap of clothes lying in front of the washer. You toss in a load and decide to go round up the clothes that accumulated yesterday. You gather those and the heap grows. Tomorrow, same heap—but you decide to gather up the clothes that accumulated yesterday. Can you see how defeating that is, not to mention the wasted time spent trying to find something to wear?

If it will take more than one day to get the laundry caught up, go to a commercial self-service laundry and you'll be finished in an hour or so. Then keep up with it.

Schedule when the wash will be done. We wash on Monday, Wednesday, Friday, and Saturday. That way the task is never overwhelming, and three days a week I don't give the laundry so much as a thought.

I have a friend who spends all day Monday washing. She heaps the clothes on the sofa or the bed (moving them to the dresser at night), and everyone folds and puts away the clothes the following Saturday. Folks, you can't do that!

The reason we get behind with laundry is because it becomes too overwhelming. One Friday I let the laundry go, so the Saturday washing was larger than usual. There it sat on the floor screaming for attention, and how I dreaded going down into the basement to get it started. Finally listening to what I preach, I decided the reason I was procrastinating was because the job seemed too big to tackle. So I broke it down into manageable portions. "Just go down there and sort," I told myself. Once I found out that what seemed to be a giant mountain of clothes was really only four smaller piles, I was all geared up and ready to go.

Another job I've learned not to procrastinate is folding. I hate folding clothes, but there's no way to avoid it unless I delegate it to someone else. Knowing that I hate to fold clothes, I've learned a few tricks that help make the job more agreeable. First, I don't wash anything unless it's turned right side out. That way, I don't have to spend even more time folding by having to turn the clothes right side out. That job is done during the sorting process (which I don't mind at all).

Next, I fold the clothes as soon as I take them out of the dryer. If you're like me, it's easier to talk yourself into spending three minutes folding one load than it is to face the whole formidable job. You know why? Because with our hectic lifestyles, three minutes are easier to come by than thirty minutes. Besides, you just may eliminate some ironing in the process.

Folding now also leads to getting the clothes put away faster. If you've tried it both ways, you know that when the clothes are folded as you go, they're usually put away in record time, simply because you don't have to wait for a block of time in which to do *all* the folding.

Putting the clothes away as soon as possible also pays dividends. It prevents rummaging, which usually leads to refolding.

"Hey, Mom! Do I have any clean jeans?"

"Yes, honey. They're just not put away yet."

So Mr. Macho heads to the laundry room and unearths everything in his path until he finds the buried treasure, leaving only stubble and ruin behind.

If your kids are folding and putting away their own laundry, stay on top of the situation and see to it that these jobs are done promptly. If you've ever found clean, folded clothes tossed into the hamper, you know what I mean.

3. *Plan and serve nutritious meals every day.*

If I were asked to give my best piece of advice to a busy mother, I'd probably say this: Be sure the house is picked up before you go to bed. Schedule the laundry and execute the schedule. And never leave the house in the morning until you know what you're having for dinner. With those three jobs under your belt, you'll have a red-letter day. Try it and see.

The food section in my planning notebook is the most time-effective tool I use in planning menus and shopping for food. Here's where I keep categorized shopping forms, menu selection sheets, freezer inventory, A-1 grocery list, and maps of my three favorite supermarkets.

It's important to shop from a list, but a categorized list is far superior to a linear list. Here's why. Items written in a column are usually jotted in the order they occur to you or the way they appear in a recipe. In other words, your list may start with hamburger and tomato soup and end with hot dogs and canned chili. If you forget the hot dogs when you're picking up the hamburger, or the chili when you select

A-1 SHOPPING LIST

Breads and Cereals _____

Health and Beauty Aids _____

Canned Goods _____

Household and Miscellaneous _____

Convenience Foods _____

Meat _____

Dairy Products and Eggs _____

Produce _____

Frozen Foods _____

Staples and Condiments _____

the soup, you have to retrace your steps and waste time traipsing back and forth through the dog food, greeting cards, panty hose, and motor oil. Another advantage of using a categorized list is that it's good no matter what store you shop at. It automatically organizes all your shopping sprees.

Whenever I'm working in the kitchen and notice we're running out of peanut butter, let's say, I turn to the first page in the food section of my planning notebook. (The first page of that section is a current shopping form.) There I write peanut butter in the staples and condiments category.

I also have a small memo pad and pencil hanging inside a convenient cupboard that the family uses and contributes to. At least once a week I transfer that list to the shopping form in my planning notebook.

The A-1 grocery list that I also keep in the food section is simply a roster of the things I never want to run out of again, such as bread, milk, ground beef, dishwasher detergent, aspirin, and Band-Aids. I keep at least two of each of these items in the house at all times—one in use and one or more in storage. As soon as the one in storage is put into use, it is immediately added to the shopping list. The A-1 list in my planning notebook serves as a reminder and helps keep the program on track.

The categorized list is a log of products we buy from time to time. Its purpose is simply to serve as a memory jogger.

The other day Jim and I were out driving around town and he said, "I have to go to K-Mart for something, but I can't remember what for." I popped open my planning notebook and scanned the categorized list. I zeroed in on the categories that apply to a store like K-Mart and read off the entire health and beauty-aid list. "No, no, no," he said to each item. Then I hit the miscellaneous category. As soon as I said, "Automatic transmission fluid," he remembered that that was what he needed to pick up. If I'm in a hurry and go to the store unprepared, the categorized list usually reminds me of everything we need (or will need sooner or later).

Next, in the food section I have what my friends call the "Twilight Zone"—store maps. Here's where I find the location of the baking chocolate, Butter Buds, marinated mushrooms, and kumquats in three different stores. If I'm at Al's Mart and can't find the Carpet Fresh, I look it up on the chart and find out that it is in aisle 9B. At Safeway it's in aisle 13A. In Jewel, Carpet Fresh is shelved along the northwest wall. What a timesaver! Now I can even send one of the kids into the store to pick something up and tell him exactly where to find it!*

With that background information, here's the best way to plan menus: Sit down and list ten or fifteen main dishes (or whole dinner menus, if you prefer) and jot down any needed ingredients on your shopping list. Also include on the list any staple items you need to have on hand for breakfasts and lunches. (I jot down the ten or fifteen meals on the back of the categorized shopping form.)

Once you've purchased everything you need, mark each jar, can, box, or bag with a large red signal dot so everyone will know it's hands-off.

Now, when you get up in the morning (or the night before), select a meal from your list that fits your mood, your time budget, and the family's schedule for that day. Then do as much as possible ahead. Defrost meat, set a salad, gather ingredients, or list instructions if the first person home is to get dinner started. Do something—anything—so you'll feel that you're in control of the situation. That alone will lift your spirits for the whole day.

4. *Keep the kitchen clean.* For a quick clean-up of the kitchen, try these time-saving techniques. If possible, start dinner after breakfast so you'll have one clean-up instead of two. Brown the meat, make dessert, steam rice, assemble the stuffing, and so forth.

---

*For copies of these lists and a more detailed discussion of each, see my book *Kitchen Organization Tips and Secrets.*

Next, clean up as you go. Whenever you prepare a meal, fill the sink with hot, soapy water even if you have a dishwasher. That one simple act eliminates a lot of cleaning time because you can toss utensils into the sink and rinse them off before any food has had a chance to petrify onto the dish. Also, have a trash bag next to your working area so you can throw wrappers and trash away as you work instead of putting things on the counter and then rounding them up again later on.

Finally, work on a piece of freezer wrap (white butcher paper that's waxed on one side). It'll catch all the drips, spills, and crumbs and will keep mixing spoons and beaters from dripping all over the counter. The freezer wrap also encourages you to confine your mess rather than scatter it throughout the kitchen!

Clean up as you go. Three simple steps that take, collectively, less than thirty seconds, but could save you thirty minutes—or more!

5. *Keep the bathroom(s) clean.*

You don't have to be a card-carrying genius to figure out how to clean a bathroom, but here are some tips to eliminate those unnecessary time wasters.

Now that you're keeping up with the laundry duties, there'll always be a covey of clean towels available for use. Right?

And since you've become the sorceress of Safeway with an organized shopping list, you'll always have a stockpile of bathroom tissue, toothpaste, and shaving cream. Right?

And certainly you've taught the kids to rinse out the sink and the bathtub and to wipe down the shower after every use. Right?

Great! Then the advice I can offer is to keep a clock in the bathroom and schedule morning bathroom time for everyone in the family.

Generally, housekeeping is a snap if you keep a few basic principles in mind:

- Be sure everything in the house has a specific place.
- Store things where they're first used and where people use them. That way, even if the object isn't put back where it belongs, at least it will be kept in the same room, a major breakthrough.
- If a storage/maintenance system isn't working, ask yourself if the item is hard to put away. If so, simplify the procedure.

We have some small plastic storage boxes with fitted lids that are the perfect size to hold decks of game cards and flash cards. They are not only the perfect size, but they stack and conserve space as well. Thinking they'd solve our card-storage problem, I bought several of the containers. But guess what? The system has failed miserably. Here's why: The kids pull out the box with the multiplication flash cards and carelessly put them back when study time is over. Later, we find a few of the cards on the living room floor, so we have to get the box out of the stack, open it up, put the cards in, close the box, and put it back in the pile. Too much work.

What's more likely to happen is this: The kids find cards lying on the living room floor. They go to the closet to put them away, but decide to put the loose cards on top of the whole stack of storage boxes (or on the shelf next to them) with the promise they'll put them in the right box the next time they have to practice their times tables. And so the system shuts down and fails.

Make your system easy to maintain. Whenever anyone complains to me that something isn't working, I can almost always guarantee that the system is too complicated. Simplify and live!*

---

*In this chapter I've just glossed over the matter of housework. If you would like to do an in-depth study of household organization, refer to my other three books.

Yes. Time management is thing management and once you have those Big Three (pick up, laundry, meals) managed and taken care of, you'll have all the time you need to go through your husband's closet!

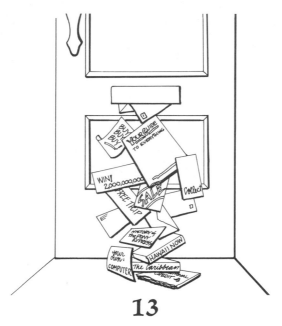

13

The Solution to Paper Pollution

Act on It, File It, or Throw It Away

There was a time, long ago, when the world was young and uncomplicated and, except for the Pony Express, comparatively devoid of mailmen. Nobody cared about magazines, letters, clearinghouse sweepstakes, coupons, bank-deposit slips, business cards, advertisements, annual reports, cash-register receipts, and dry-cleaning claim checks. In short, nobody cared about Paperwork. The word was lowercased then rather than a registered trademark like Xerox or American Express. Paperwork was merely an event, not a spectacular. Certainly it was not the Serious Business it is today.

Nowadays, though, with something called "mass communications" and as members of the global village, we are daily defending ourselves against a battering-ram of paper.

We hoard, collect, stash, stack, and squirrel away everything from appliance booklets to articles heralding the benefits of furniture made from zebrawood.

And what do we do with it all? Well, we could always
bundle it up and use it as a doorstop or as a blunt weapon.
But for those with the stamina to plow through, a system is
the solution to paper pollution.

Paper is not as frightening as its imposing appearance
would have you believe. Basically, there are only three things
you can do with any scrap of paper you come across: throw
it away, file it, or take some kind of action on it. That's not
so hard, is it?

Whenever you encounter a piece of paper, your first decision should be whether or not you need it. Respond to the
following statements with *true* or *false*:

- This item would be very easy to replace were I to
  throw it away.
- Nothing terrible would happen if I were to throw it
  away.
- No one is really interested in this information.
- I can transfer the information to my planning note-
  book or family organizer.
- This information has become obsolete or outdated.
- I have not needed or referred to this information for
  years.

If any of these statements are true, then you can safely
toss away the paper or papers in question.

Once you decide what stays and what goes, run, don't
walk, to the nearest office supply store and stock up on the
following supplies:

- 3 letter-sized expanding files with 12 pockets each (or
  use portable hanging files)
- 2 expanding check files
- file folders

- 1 two- or four-drawer file cabinet (or make do for now with portable file boxes or cardboard boxes)

Here's what goes where:

1. Use one of the large expanding files for the household goods information file. Appliance booklets, warranties, and information about the furniture, musical instruments, draperies, carpeting, stereo, lawn mower, snowblower, tools, and so forth, goes here. Information on the trombone goes in the T pocket. G holds the barbecue grill booklet. S keeps the stereo information and the snowblower instruction manual and warranty.

Don't worry about alphabetizing any further than the first letter. These items are needed so infrequently that there's no sense wasting time overfiling them. When you need the refrigerator booklet to find out how to clean the coils, pull out the R's and in less than thirty seconds you'll have the information in your hands.

2. Put untried recipes in another large expanding file. Designate each pocket in the file to keep a certain food category: appetizers, beverages, cakes, cookies, desserts, main dishes, vegetables, and so on. When you rip out a delicious-sounding recipe from the paper or receive one from a friend, toss it in the designated pocket. When you want it, you'll be able to find it quickly. And if you want to pore over some new main-dish ideas, they'll be organized and ready for your perusal.

When a recipe is tried and enjoyed, put it in your file of tried-and-true recipes or mount it in a cookbook or magnetic photo album.

3. Financial records go into another expanding file. Each pocket represents a month of the year. Here again many people waste time and space setting up files for every company they do business with. When bills are paid, they spend fifteen to twenty minutes putting the Amex statement into the American Express folder, the Sears statement into the Sears folder and so on. (Or they leave the stuff mounded on

top of the dresser for now.) Instead, why not sit down once a month, pay the bills, and put all the statements into a monthly pocket. In one fell swoop the filing is done. (Working papers on tax matters can be held in a separate pocket or pulled out at the end of the year.)

Now, if there's a question regarding a payment (which doesn't happen too often) just grab the contents of that month's pocket and you'll have the information in less than a minute. Remember, simple systems reduce clutter and are easy to maintain. This expanding file is stored at the end of the year and replaced by a new one on January 1.

4. File cancelled checks and bank statements in one of the expanding check files, filed by month—after they're reconciled, of course. (This file too will be stored at the end of the year and replaced by a new one on January 1.)

5. File coupons in the other expanding check file by categories. Label each pocket accordingly. For added convenience and to insure that the coupons will be used, keep the file in the car. P.S. All fast food coupons should be kept in the car too.

Next put the financial records, cancelled checks, and household goods information file in one file drawer. In the front of this drawer, finish out your active file with file folders labeled using any headings you deem necessary. Here are the most common categories:

- Car information
- Club information (book club, record club, craft club)
- Correspondence
- Education records (schools attended, degrees, awards, activities, transcripts, information about relevant seminars and technical instruction)
- Employment records (resumes, letters of recommendation, previous employers, health benefit information, insurance programs, personal office information)
- Credit card information

- Health and immunization records
- Insurance policies (unless you're keeping them in a safe-deposit box)
- Product information
- Property
- Restaurants (menus for take-out, critical reviews)
- Safe-deposit box inventory and extra key
- Services (lawn care, housekeeping, paper hanger, electrician, building contractor)
- Travel (maps, hotel information, restaurants, tourist information, rent-a-car information)

Remember, don't overfile. Use broad, general descriptions. A folder labeled Vehicles is better than a separate folder each for the car, the motorcycle, the boat, the snowmobile, the ATV, and the moped. A few fat files are better than a bunch of skinny ones. If a file is growing too thick and cumbersome, break it down into logical, easy-to-find groups. For example, if the travel folder is ignoring its boundaries, divide it into Travel—foreign, Travel—USA West, Travel—USA East.

Never name a file using an adjective or adverb, unless the tag word means something to you. Change Cute Party Ideas to simply Parties or Entertainment.

Don't file paper clips. If several pages must be secured together, use a stapler. Paper clips can catch other nonrelated papers and refile them permanently.

And finally, do not set up a miscellaneous file.

In the second file drawer, set up a reference file. Here's where you keep that article on the zebrawood; the decorating article you ripped out of *Better Homes and Gardens*; a booklet entitled "How to Childproof Your Home"; a leaflet about the care and feeding of a Ficus Benjamina, and so forth. Here are some suggestions of possible categories for your reference file:

- Beauty—hair care and make-up techniques

- Decoration—interior decorating ideas, landscape designs, plans for building a deck
- Fashion—outfit ideas, tips for accessorizing, how to buy proper fitting undergarments
- Gardening (indoor and outdoor)—how to keep the rubber tree alive and well, windowbox gardens, planning a garden plot
- Health—exercises, articles on drug abuse, diet information, guide to prenatal care, notes from lecture on sleep, fatigue, and energy
- Hobbies—If you're a project person you may need a separate folder or drawer for each specific area of interest
- Science—articles about avalanches, Great Blue Herons, volcanic eruptions, and space travel

This is just a skeleton list that will vary greatly, depending upon your personal interests and needs. If you collect information on antiques, photography, yoga, or have a collection of children's stories, sheet music, poetry, or visual aids, then you'll probably need to include categorical files to accommodate each of them.

Be sure to keep the file headings broad and generic, and divide them only when they become unwieldy. If your health file is being overrun with articles and information on exercise, remove them and set up an exercise file.

Personally, I have an enormous file that contains over a thousand articles, visual aids for teaching children, music, craft projects, and so on. Because of the size of this collection I now use a numerical filing system that I detailed in *Confessions of an Organized Housewife*. Generally, though, the subject file that I've described here is more than adequate for the average collector. It's easy to set up and permits quick retrieval of stored information.

With just a few more accoutrements, you'll finally have a place for every single scrap of paper that will ever come your way.

You need a basket, box, or other type of container to hold things that need to be filed and another container to serve as an in-basket. As soon as the mail is received, immediately toss out the junk. Put bills to pay, letters to answer, magazine subscriptions to renew, statements to reconcile— anything that requires action—in the in-box. (Put things that must be referred to the children in their in/out baskets. See chapter 6.)

Now, just for fun, let's pretend the following stack of paper is sitting on your dining room table. I'll tell you exactly how I would deal with each item.

- *Family Circle* magazine
- Tickets to a John Denver concert
- Child of the Week poster highlighting your son (the poster is on butcher paper and is bigger than he is)
- An article reprint on time management sent to you from Day-Timers
- A trade journal
- Corrected spelling test
- Credit card receipt from J. C. Penney
- Order form for a replacement tone arm for your preschoolers' new record player
- A shopping list
- Craft mail-order catalog
- Proof-of-purchase points from Masters of the Universe packages
- Notes from the lecture "Lowering Your Setpoint"
- Original story "James Bond Goes Bowling," written by your seventh grader
- Receipt for the shoes you bought for your daughter (she wasn't with you, and you need to keep the receipt just in case you have to return or exchange the shoes)
- Flyer you picked up in the bookstore announcing a seminar on stress to be given at the local community center

- A newspaper picture of the seventh grade honor students
- Dry cleaning and photo claim checks
- Cartoon snowman you saved from the newspaper (you may want to copy it for a poster, an invitation, or a Sunday School visual aid)
- A message for your husband
- Car insurance ad you tore out of the paper (you want to call the company to get a quote when your insurance comes due in three months)

Okay, here we go.

1. *Family Circle magazine*: Whenever I'm reading a magazine, I dog-ear articles I want to keep. Then, when I'm finished with the periodical, I rip out the marked pages, staple complete articles together, and put them in my to-file basket. Whenever you're reading something that you're going to file later on, jot a key word or two in the upper right-hand corner of the article. Days or even weeks later when you get around to filing the piece, you can put the material in the right file without having to re-read it.

Magazines are usually 80 percent advertising and 20 percent information, so it's generally wasteful to keep the entire book. When I come across an old magazine, I quickly check for dog-eared pages. If there are none, I toss the magazine away without double checking to see if there's anything I missed. There are, however, some entire magazines I do save. In that case, I staple an index card to the upper right-hand corner of the magazine cover and note the subject and page number of the articles (or crafts) I want to remember.

If you have a stack of magazines sitting around that you're waiting to go through, you'll feel less burdened if you'll just toss them out. Besides, magazine indexes and back copies are available at most libraries. Let the librarians do the organizing and storing—they are equipped for it!

2. *Tickets to John Denver concert*: Be sure the concert date, time, and location are recorded in your calendar. Put

the tickets in a zippered pouch in the back of your planning notebook or in a file folder marked Pending. Make a note in your planning notebook where the tickets are stored.

3. *"Child of the Week" poster*: Take a close-up photograph of your child standing next to the poster, and after you've displayed the actual poster for a week or two, throw it out. (You'll still have the photo.)

4. *Time-management article*: If it seems to be worth reading, read it. If not, throw it out. If you want to save it, file it under a general term (such as Organizing) in the reference file.

5. *Trade journal*: If you do a lot of reading, designate a spot where you put things you want to read—nightstand, magazine rack, large basket, briefcase, cardboard box, and so on. If things start stacking up, it's time to cancel some subscriptions.

6. *Corrected spelling test*: Throw it out. (This is easier to do if you do it on garbage day when the truck is sitting in front of your house!)

7. *Credit card receipt*: File it in the financial records file according to date, or toss it into the to-file basket.

8. *Order form for tone arm*: This goes into the household goods file under R for record player. When the tone arm needs to be replaced, the order form will be ready and waiting.

9. *Shopping list*: All shopping lists should be included in your planning notebook, not on a floating piece of paper. Transfer the list to the planning notebook and throw the original list away. (See chapter 12.)

10. *Craft mail-order catalog*: Scan quickly (if it's small) to see if there's anything you want to order; if not, throw it out or store it with your craft books, other catalogs, or magazines. (Be sure to toss it out when the next edition arrives.)

11. *Proof-of-purchase points from Masters of the Universe toys*: If the kids are saving the proofs, keep these in their junk drawers. If you're saving the points to get a refund

or a discount on another toy purchase, file them in the expanding file where you keep coupons. (Label one section Proofs of Purchase.) This approach, by the way, is only for a casual couponer-refunder.

12. *Lecture notes*: Put these in the reference file under Health.

13. *"James Bond Goes Bowling"*: Every child needs to have a safe place for keeping such items as original stories, artwork, past report cards, and photos. These can be put in scrapbooks, files, or photo albums.

Each of our children has a covered box, which is stored in the basement, where we keep such treasures. However, since I'm not the kind of person who enjoys running downstairs every day to file things away, I keep a dishpan for each child upstairs in the linen closet (or on a bedroom closet shelf), and anything we want to keep forever is tossed into the child's dishpan. Then, once a year I take the dishpans downstairs and put each child's collection into a dated envelope and put the envelope in the covered box.

14. *Receipt for shoes*: Keep this in a zippered pouch in the back of your planning notebook. If the shoes fit and no exchange is necessary, throw the receipt away.

15. *Flyer about stress lecture*: Open your calendar to the date of the seminar, and record all pertinent information. Turn to the running to-do list in your planning notebook and write "register for seminar before (date)." Throw the flyer away.

16. *Newspaper picture of your son, the honor student*: Put the clipping in his "keep forever" dishpan. (You may want to make a few photocopies first, though.)

17. *Dry cleaning and photo claim checks*: Put these in the zippered pouch in the back of your planning notebook.

18. *Cartoon snowman*: File in reference file under Art— Ideas.

19. *Message for your husband*: Jot in the family organizer and throw the original message away.

20. *Car insurance ad*: File this information with your car-insurance policy in the active file. Then turn ahead three months in your calendar and make a note to call that particular insurance company. Be sure to indicate that the information is filed with your current policy.

What about business cards and keeping track of various names and addresses? Instead of using an address book, I use a card file. Why? Because I find that it's easier to keep the cards in alphabetical order in a card file than in a linear listing in an address book. Also, address books eventually wear out and need to be entirely recopied—not so with a card file. And finally, there's room on the card to record tidbits about the person or family, such as names of children, food likes and dislikes, and ideas for gifts.

I save business cards only if I'm sure we'll need them in the future. I staple them to an index card and file them yellow-page style. For example, John Brown, plumber, is filed under P for plumber; Ed White, wholesale tool dealer, is filed under T for tools. Unless I remember the person's name, I file by category.

Yes, I know what to do with paper, but there's still one thing I just can't seem to figure out. Why don't those seventeen subscription renewal cards in my *Ladies' Home Journal* fall out in the mail rather than on my living room floor?

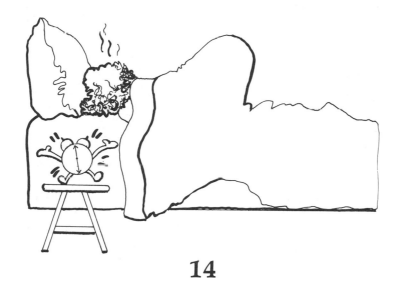

14

Born Tired 'n Still Restin'

How to Get Up and Going

"The bed is a bundle of paradoxes: we go to it with reluctance, yet we quit it with regret; we make up our minds every night to leave it early, but we make up our bodies every morning to keep it late." Caleb C. Colton said this early in the nineteenth century. Today it's better known as the Fizzle Phenomenon.

It's 6:00 A.M. and the blast furnace voice of your alarm clock blares you out of a dream. Presto, your brain turns to ectoplasm, your eyelids suddenly have the relative density of manhole covers, and your paralyzed limbs are a quivering mass of gelatin.

What happened to that indomitable zeal you felt last night? You vowed you'd get an early start this morning, perhaps to do some jogging or to spend a quiet hour alone. Slowly the thought dissolves. Nothing short of a hydraulically operated forklift could get you out of bed now. So you hit the snooze button and save your zeal for tomorrow or maybe the next day.

By the time the alarm yowls again, dull, muddled, and showing little sign of improvement, you squint at the clock. Faced with unspeakable consequences should you choose to sleep another minute, you begrudgingly assume a vertical position.

Yes, bunky, you have blown it again. (That from my memoirs.)

So here, direct from the proving ground (my bed) are ten tried-and-true methods to help you peel the mattress off your back.

1. Get a good night's sleep. It's much easier to get up in the morning when you've slept well the night before. Even under optimum conditions, it's hard to face the day. And when you've had a fitful night's sleep, tossing and turning, waking up every two or three hours to check the clock, it's nigh unto impossible to roll out at reveille. If you suspect your early morning languor is due in part to poor sleep habits, try some of these "sleeping pills":

- Straighten the house before bed. Repose is peaceful when you lie down in a peaceful, orderly atmosphere. You feel more content, satisfied, and finished with your day's work. And isn't it easier to turn out of bed when you can see the floor beneath you? Sure it is. Who wants to get up to yesterday's work and start the morning one day behind?

- Set an alarm clock. Did you think an alarm clock could help you get to sleep? Whenever I hit the sack and say, "I don't need to set the alarm, I know I'll get up on time," I'm setting myself up for a restless night. Every hour or so I waken to look at the clock and see if I've overslept. Set the clock and let *it* do the worrying for you. If you're afraid it won't go off, set a second alarm as a back-up. If you're afraid the electricity will fail during the night, use a wind-up model.

- Don't eat a big meal just before retiring. I won't pretend to be knowledgeable about the physiology of human digestion and its effect on sleep, but I've read, heard, and experienced enough to believe the statement is true.
- Have tomorrow planned. You'll be on top of things and in control, and that pleasant sensation of satisfaction will soothe you into a blissful state of sleep. Then, as an added incentive, when you wake up you'll have an immediate jump on the day.

2. Just open your eyes. Tell yourself, "I'm not going to get up. I'm only going to open my eyes." Now, that's not so bad, is it?

3. Sit up. If you're really well self-disciplined, this one may work well for you. Just sit up and keep sleeping—if you can.

4. Use other people. Tell your husband to encourage your attempts at early rising. For example, when Jim says, "Aw, come on. You can sleep for thirty more minutes," I say, "Mmmm, it's so warm here. Maybe I'll just zzzzzzz." But when he says something like, "Boy, you're a trooper getting up this early," I practically bolt out of bed. Here we go again with communicating. Tell someone else what your plan is and why you need to get up. Ask the supporting party to encourage rather than coddle.

5. Wake up and worry. I know, Dr. Hans Selje, the Boghwan of stress, would probably not approve of this idea were he alive to object. But it works, nevertheless. What kept you awake the night before? Wake up and worry about it now. Besides, at night you're helpless, but in the morning you can do something about it.

And what, pray tell, is there to worry about? Somebody's grades, finances, the leaky roof, business (or lack of), the stupid thing you said at the party last night, nuclear activism, tax audits, the employee you have to fire, the birthday card you forgot to send to your mother, political hostages, the fender you crumpled, the backlog of work heaped on your desk, the state of your three-bedlam house. Should I continue?

Wake up and worry—and once the desire for sleep has flown, arise and shine!

6. Make early appointments. When I have early-morning phone appointments coming into the office at seven o'clock, I'm up, dressed, and out the door before I've even had a chance to feel sorry for myself.

Schedule the earliest appointments available with the doctor, dentist, lawyer, accountant, hairdresser, manicurist, tanning salon, or whatever, and use that extrinsic motivation to force yourself out of bed. Or, better yet, schedule early appointments at your house. (Now there's something else you can worry about.)

Sign up for an early aerobics class or gather a bunch of friends who are interested in an early morning run. You'll not only be surrounded by similarly motivated people, but the structure may be just what you need (in addition to some healthy embarrassment if you slack off).

7. Promise yourself a nap, or an early bedtime if you're working. I use this one nearly every day. And once in a while I take myself up on the promise. It's important that this not be merely a trick because it'll never work. But I know full well that if I'm exhausted come midday I'll take a nap, if I'm home, or get to bed early that night. Just knowing I'll make good on my promise, I trust myself and get out of bed. It's a law of physics: a body at rest tends to stay at rest and one that's in motion tends to stay in motion. And usually, once I've been in motion for ten minutes, all desire for sleep has passed.

8. Set alarms. Alarms, as I mentioned above, can contribute to a sound night's sleep and, of course, they get you up in the morning. If you're a stubborn case, don't use a

clock radio (the music will lull you back to sleep) and don't have one of those fancy models with a snooze button or other amenities.

What you need is a blaring, jolting, buzzing, shrieking clock that's at least ten steps from the bed. If you can, put the clock close to the shower so you can shut off the alarm, hop in the shower, and enjoy its pulsating heat. (An immediate reward.) Or, put the alarm in the kitchen, and as long as you're up, you might just as well get started on breakfast.

9. Vividly imagine yourself doing something. Just lie there with your eyes closed and imagine that you're dressed and ready for the day. How do you look? How do you feel? Next, picture yourself performing some particular task: fixing a gourmet breakfast, calling on a client, shopping, going for a job interview, writing a letter. The point is to see yourself in action while activating your brain. This one takes some concentration but it's easy, and you don't have to open your eyes until you're no longer comatose. I promise that you'll be ready for action within five minutes.

10. Reward yourself. What do you have to look forward to today or this weekend? There has to be a pot of gold at the end of the rainbow, and it must be realistic.

A while back I was reading an article about motivating yourself to exercise. Naturally, rewards were one group of motivators. So, the writer suggested, "If you get to exercise class today, you deserve a new leotard." Pictured alongside the article was a shopping bag stuffed with leg warmers, leotards, and bodysuits, flanked by a credit card, some cash, and a receipt for $180.00!

Now that makes as much sense as saying, "I went to exercise class today, so on the way home I'll stop off for a few Big Macs, a chocolate shake, a large carton of fries, a cherry turnover, and a box of McDonaldland cookies."

If you haven't done so already, start working on that reward list I outlined in chapter 3. That way you'll be assured of choosing a reward that motivates you—not to mention one you can afford!

If you're not a morning person and you're not a night person and your family wonders, "When are you a person?" for heaven's sake wake up and worry, reward yourself, open your eyes, promise yourself a nap, do *something*.

15

Chipping Off the Old Block

How to Get Started

Every morning we awaken to another round of housework and homework, deadlines and diapers, time clocks and tedium, never to be saved by the bell. Yes, every day we get up and do today what we didn't even want to do yesterday. But get up we do.

So, what's the bottom line? Where to start. I have spoken to thousands of women (millions through the media of TV and radio), and the question I'm asked most often is, "Where do I start?" Forget the Halls of Montezuma. This plaintive cry is heard from the kitchens of Cleveland to the shores of Shanghai. We all know we must start—we should start—but where?

Perhaps you've started before, were unsuccessful, and fear trying it again. This time will be different. Why? Because most of us (myself included) have started in a haphazard manner with only vague expectations.

The laundry is heaped in a voluminous mass next to the washing machine, and you decide to get it caught up. About halfway through the first rinse cycle, someone needs a ride to soccer practice. On the way home you stop off at the store for a loaf of bread, a container of milk, and a pound of butter. Arriving home, you toss another load in the washer and start dinner. Then it's back to soccer practice to pick up the team. Finish dinner. Help with homework. Do the dishes. What about the laundry? Well, if aging is acceptable for USDA beef and cheese, then why not let the laundry ferment for one more day? And so it goes. You wave your dish towel at half-mast and surrender your good intentions.

So why will this time be different? Because this time you're going to start in the right place and in a logical, sequential, and predetermined manner. Here's how I jumped off the merry-go-round. No matter what household task will suffer, you must take time to sit down with a piece of paper and a pen and make a list of possible starting points.

To get your list underway, answer the following questions:

1. What is giving you "that feeling"? Have you ever had "that feeling"? If you haven't experienced it, "that feeling" is when you wake up in the morning and notice the shower is beginning to grow. You open the crisper in the refrigerator and discover that the green peppers have liquefied. You glance at the stove top and just for fun write your name in the splattered, congealed grease. (One woman told me, "I don't care if you write your name as long as you don't put the *year!*") That, my friend, is "that feeling." Write its cause on your paper.

2. What is bothering you about your environment?

3. What household tasks or projects are you procrastinating?

4. What projects have you started but haven't finished?

5. Would you let someone walk through your home unattended? If not, list anything you'd be embarrassed for someone to see.

6. What causes most of your interruptions—such as telephone calls, children wanting food or drinks, people looking for things?

7. Is something a source of unnecessary contention in your home?

8. Why are you reading this book?

I cannot stress enough the importance of making this physical list. Here's why. In your mind you know the answers to each one of these questions. Consciously or not, you are constantly reminding yourself of those uncompleted tasks, feeling the weight of their burden, mentally reprimanding yourself for not performing those duties, and generally feeling guilty, overwhelmed, and hopeless. In short, what we have here is a whole bunch of unresolved stress.

You cannot control this stress unless you can physically see it, prioritize it, and objectively decide on a course of action.

Here's what my list looked like when I hit bottom twelve years ago:

- laundry
- toys
- paperwork
- newspapers everywhere
- scrapbooks for the kids
- windows need washing
- basement stuff needs to be categorized and organized into boxes
- implement an exercise program
- need to do more reading
- learn to crochet
- start a filing system
- should start using a calendar or reminder book
- start planning menus

- pick up the house at least 3 times a week
- bedroom doors stick
- cracked window in living room
- bathroom needs repainting
- go through pile of magazines

(Actually, the list was longer, but I think you get the idea.)

Frequently people who haven't participated in this exercise shy away from it for fear of becoming too discouraged by the potential length of the list. I'm always too polite to tell those folks that they're just making excuses—but that's all they're doing. Excuses are retarding! Go ahead and make the list.

Once your list is itemized, it's time to get started. Pick up your list and put a check mark beside anything that has to do with picking up, laundry, meals, kitchen, or bathrooms. If anything is causing unnecessary interruptions, put a check mark by it. If anything on your list is causing contention in your home, put a check mark by it. Is something on the list making you feel as if a large piece of farm equipment is in your stomach? Put a check mark by it.

Now, look over the list. The items with the most checks win. You have just discovered the best place for *you* to start. You've isolated the most stress-inducing, time-wasting tasks in your life right now, and to eliminate them will bring instant satisfaction, higher self-esteem, and a desire for more victories. Trust me. Once you've tasted success, the snowball will begin rolling up the hill!

Hang on to your list, but don't prioritize it. After you've dispensed with the first Big One, go back to the list, re-evaluate it, and pick project number two. This list can now become the birth of that running to-do list I've been talking about for several chapters. Whenever you think of yet another thing you have to do, just add it to the list.

Now that you know *where* to start, let's talk about *how* to start. The first question you should ask yourself is, "Do I have enough information to proceed?" In other words, do you know how to do the job you've selected as your starting point? Do you know how to set up a filing system? Do you know how to keep those bedroom doors from sticking? Do you know what to do with school papers so the kitchen counter will stay clean?

If not, find out. Talk to experts or friends who can give you the answers you need. Read books or articles on the subject. For example, my books can teach you in great detail how to set up a file, clear up the school papers, and organize a laundry schedule, but I'd be hard-pressed to tell you how to paint and paper the bathroom or unstick the bedroom doors. You'll have to look elsewhere for those answers.

Gathering information, if necessary, is always step number one. Step number two is to determine your *modus operandi*. What's your plan of attack? How will you accomplish the task? Here is an example from my own experience:

After tackling the laundry, the toys, the closets, and the cupboards, the next thing on my list was to set up a reference file. I wanted to use a system that would allow me to file things away and retrieve them quickly. That was my goal, but I had no idea how to do it. I talked to many people about their systems. I read articles and books, and finally an old college textbook gave me what I considered to be the best option. With that know-how, I was then able to plan my work. Here are the steps I followed:

1. Purchase file folders, index cards, and alphabetical file guides.

2. Purchase inexpensive file cabinet. Read classified ads.

3. Spend one hour a day (Monday through Friday during the baby's nap time) filing.

I stuck to my plan, and in one month the file was completed and functioning smoothly.

In a nutshell, here's the system:

- Choose a starting point.
- Gather needed information.

- Plan the project.
- Stick to the plan.

I know, I'm sneaky. I sort of slipped number four in there, didn't I. There's always a catch. I suppose any plan in the world would work if you were consistent with it. Here are a few tips to help you maintain your resolve:

- Put blinders on.
- Concentrate on your high-priority task and don't be sidetracked by other activities.
- Keep starting over and don't give up.

When I got down to the item on my list that read "start using a calendar or reminder book," I was initially very excited and anxious to add this professional dimension to my life. For two weeks I meticulously recorded all dates, deadlines, and appointments, and made careful notes about upcoming events and assignments. Then, gradually, my enthusiasm waned and days went by with nary an observation. I started over, stopped again, and started over. Finally my somewhat blemished bout of determination led by degrees to the formation of one of the best habits I have yet acquired.

Thank goodness you can keep starting over until you get it right! It's never too late. If you mess up, just start over. The single reason that I finally got organized was this: I never stopped starting over. I kept everlastingly at it—and I still do.

16

Springing the Time Trap

Make Yours a Singing House

Start spreading the news: this timid time manager has been trimmed into a tiger. Just look at yourself—you finished this entire book! I know you can do it; you can spring the time trap once and for all. And if business acquaintances ask you how you did it, just hand them a copy of this book and say, "These same principles can be translated into use at the office, too." (Ahhhhhh, sweet revenge.)

I'm frequently asked where I get all my energy. I learned a long time ago that natural energy drives are released when we do what we enjoy. So, I spend my spare hours doing the things that bring me the most joy and satisfaction. You can too.

You can receive one or two extra hours a day to use as

you choose just by applying the ideas you've read in this book. How will you spend the time?

You have the motivation, but now it's time to pay the price. Won't you set up a planning notebook and begin using it every day? Won't you choose just a few goals and begin working on them now? I know you'd do it for money. And you'd do it for the sake of a loved one, wouldn't you? Then won't you do it for your own happiness? The best way to rid yourself of depressed feelings is to take action on something that really matters. Try it and see.

I have enjoyed spending this time with you, and I hope that you will experience the good feelings of peace and security that enter your life when things are organized and you're in control of your time.

In closing, may I share with you a quaint but charming story I've loved for years, by May Potter. It best describes my hopes and dreams for you and yours. I wish for you a singing house.

The Singing House

I tied the napkin around Fred's neck and placed before him his glass of orange juice, his cereal, his big glass of foamy milk. In my opinion, I classified among the superior mothers whose children are brought up in the approved manner of an enlightened day.

Fred ate it all dutifully and then slipped down from his chair.

"Now can I go over to Jimmy's, Mother?" he asked.

"But Fred," I remonstrated, "you were over there yesterday and the day before. Why not have Jimmy come here today?"

"Oh, he wouldn't want to." Fred's lip quivered in spite of his six years of manhood. "Please, Mother."

"Why do you like Jimmy's house better than ours, son?" I pursued. It came to me suddenly that Fred and all his companions were always wanting to go to Jimmy's house.

"Why," he explained hesitatingly, "it's 'cause—it's 'cause Jimmy's house is a singing house."

"A singing house?" I questioned. "Now what do you mean by that?"

"Well," Fred was finding it hard to explain, "Jimmy's mother hums when she sews; and Annie-in-the-kitchen, she sings when she cuts out cookies; and Jimmy's daddy always whistles when he comes home." Fred stopped a moment and added, "Their curtains are rolled clear up and there's flowers in the windows. All the boys like Jimmy's house, Mother."

"You may go, son," I said quickly. I wanted him out of the way so I could think.

I looked around my house. Everyone told me how lovely it was. There were oriental rugs. We were paying for them in installments. That was why there wasn't any Annie-in-the-kitchen here. We were paying for the overstuffed furniture and the car that way also. Perhaps that was why Fred's daddy didn't whistle when he came into the house.

I put on my hat and went over to Jimmy's house, even though it was ten o'clock and Saturday morning. It came to me that Mrs. Burton would not mind being interrupted in the middle of the morning. She never seemed to be in a hurry. She met me at the door with a towel around her head.

"Oh, come in. I have just finished the living room. No, indeed, you are not interrupting. I'll just take off this head-dress and be right in."

While I waited, I looked around. The rugs were almost threadbare; the curtains, dotted Swiss, ruffled and tied back; the furniture, old and scarred but freshened with new cre-tonnes. A table with a bright cover held a number of old magazines. In the window were hanging baskets of ivy and wandering Jew, while a bird warbled from his cage hanging in the sun. Homey, that was the effect.

The kitchen door was open and I saw Jerry, the baby, sitting on the clean linoleum, watching Annie as she pinched together the edges of an apple pie. She was singing. . . .

Mrs. Burton came in smiling. "Well," she asked, "what is it? For I know you came for something; you are such a busy woman."

"Yes," I said abruptly, "I came to see what a singing house is like."

Mrs. Burton looked puzzled. "Why, what do you mean?"

"Fred says he loves to come here because you have a singing house. I begin to see what he means."

"What a wonderful compliment!" Mrs. Burton's face flushed. "But of course my house doesn't compare with yours. Everyone says you have the loveliest house in town."

"But it isn't a singing house," I objected. "Tell me how you came to have one."

"Well," smiled Mrs. Burton, "if you really want to know. You see, John doesn't make much. I don't think he ever will. He isn't that type. We have to cut somewhere, and we decided on nonessentials. I am not a very strong person, and when Jerry came, we decided Annie was an essential if the children were to have a cheeerful mother. Then there are books, magazines, and music. These are things the children can keep inside. They can't be touched by fire or reverse so we decided they were essentials. Of course, good wholesome food is another essential. The children's clothes are very simple. But when all these things are paid for, there doesn't seem to be much left for rugs and furniture. We don't go into debt if we can avoid it. However, we are happy," she concluded.

"I see," I said thoughtfully. I looked over at Jimmy and Fred in the corner. They had manufactured a train out of match boxes and were loading it with wheat. They were scattering it a good deal, but wheat is clean and wholesome.

I went home. My oriental rugs looked faded. I snapped my curtains to the top of the windows, but the light was subdued as it came through the silken draperies. My house was not a singing house. I determined to make it sing.

Index

For more information on

- *Confessions of an Organized Homemaker*
- *Confessions of a Happily Organized Family*
- *Kitchen Organization Tips and Secrets*
- How to get a complete planning notebook
- How to get a cleaning cart
- How to sponsor a Deniece Schofield seminar or speaking engagement

Write to

Deniece Schofield
PO Box 214
Cedar Rapids, IA 52406